# OFFICE
# ARCHITECTURE + DESIGN

MASTERPIECES

LARA MENZEL

# OFFICE
# ARCHITECTURE + DESIGN

BRAUN

# PREFACE. VORWORT. PRÉFACE.

The progress of the digital revolution, job diversification, and the ever-increasing demands placed on office buildings in terms of their configuration and technology, have all significantly altered the task of office construction in the course of the last decades. An added driving force behind this sea change is the gradual abandonment of large-capacity company offices and the scores of post-war office buildings in sore need of renovation. Sophisticated ventilation technologies and energy concepts are quickly becoming the company's public face, and these innovations often go hand in hand with corporate design. New office types, such as the combi office, appear next to traditional kinds that have been with us since antiquity, like the group and the cell office. Psychological studies have repeatedly confirmed the significant value for the business sector of creating a workspace that puts employees at ease. Communications research has pointed out the workflow advantages of flexibility and spontaneity, subverting entrenched Taylorist models. Finally, ecological thinking and state-of-the-art concepts have joined forces to eradicate the "stale office air". The office building and its inner workings, its spaces, and the management of information, processes, and monies both private and public which goes on within, are all at the center of this book. Representation is a challenge that today stands at the forefront of

Digitale Revolution, Mehrfachtätigkeit und wachsende Erfordernisse an Gestaltung und Technik von Bürobauten haben in den letzten Jahrzehnten die Bauaufgabe Büro signifikant verändert. Eine weitere entscheidende Rolle spielen der abnehmende Bedarf an ausgedehnten Büroflächen sowie der große Bestand an Bürogebäuden aus der Nachkriegszeit, die dringend umgebaut werden müssen. Raffinierte Belüftungstechniken und Energiekonzepte entwickeln sich schnell zum Aushängeschild des Unternehmens, und diese Innovationen gehen häufig mit dem Corporate Design einher. Neue Bürotypen wie das Kombibüro stehen Seite an Seite mit traditionellen, seit jeher bekannten Formen des Gruppen- oder Einzelbüros. Wiederholt haben psychologische Untersuchungen die Bedeutung eines behaglichen Arbeitsplatzes für das Unternehmen herausgestellt. Die Kommunikationsforschung belegt die Vorteile von Flexibilität und Spontaneität für den Arbeitsablauf und untergräbt damit die etablierten taylorschen Arbeitsmodelle. Schließlich sind ökologisches Denken und dem neuesten Stand der Wissenschaft entsprechende Konzepte gemeinsam gegen den „Büromief" angegangen. Der Bürobau und sein Betrieb, seine Räume und das Management von Informationen, Abläufen stehen im Mittelpunkt dieses Buches. Bei der Planung eines Bürogebäudes ist die Präsentation heute die schwierigste Aufgabe, da

L'évolution récente du monde de l'entreprise – révolution numérique, diversification des tâches, exigences technologiques toujours plus grandes – a profondément modifié le travail des architectes chargé de concevoir des immeubles commerciaux. D'autant plus que les grands bureaux ouverts cèdent progressivement la place aux bureaux individuels, et que de nombreux bâtiments construits après la Seconde Guerre mondiale doivent maintenant être rénovés.

Les entreprises privilégient désormais les concepts énergétiques sophistiqués qui valorisent leur image. De nouveaux types de bureaux, notamment le « bureau combiné », viennent compléter des structures plus traditionnelles, tandis que des études psychologiques récentes montrent l'importance capitale de l'atmosphère au travail sur la productivité des employés, et que des recherches sur la communication soulignent les avantages de la flexibilité et de la spontanéité – deux concepts qui abolissent les anciens modèles tayloristes. Par ailleurs, des approches écologistes tirent parti de la technologie moderne pour améliorer la ventilation des bureaux et éradiquer les mauvaises odeurs qui y régnaient jadis. Le présent ouvrage est entièrement consacré aux immeubles de bureaux, à leur financement et à leur fonctionnement interne. Notons que le besoin de

the office's tasks, since its functions inadvertently include administration of the company or government agency that runs it. It goes without saying that "the office" often finds itself sharing boundaries with spaces of various functionality within one structural entity (for example, a building may house offices, a hotel, as well as residential units). Some projects even occupy this boundary exactly – for example, spaces accommodating e-commerce. Functional centers and areas section the office into task-oriented spaces, which can also be adapted to a different function quickly (just-in-time office).

The discovery of the "human capital" leads to the next approximation of the ideal work space for employers and employees. The "sick building" syndrome prompted interest on the part of the employer, solely for economical reasons, to seek ways to improve workplace quality of life. The finding that casual meetings in informal zones, unplanned conversations throughout the work process during errand-running, and spontaneous knowledge exchange all have a cost-saving effect, loosen and relax the work space territory. Access spaces turn from a cost unit to valuable social hubs, whose use is encouraged by walkways and bridges winding through the building. The "business club" experiments with a new layout, where contrasting spaces, including lounges, create an environment for all processes and meetings for a predominantly telecommuting staff.

*Masterpieces Office Architecture + Design* attaches to the success of the publication *Offices,* with the same focus on office architecture worldwide and with new perspectives of the lastingness and ecological building pointed out.

auch der Betreiber des Gebäudes – das Unternehmen oder die staatliche Einrichtung – zu berücksichtigen ist. Es versteht sich von selbst, dass „Büros" innerhalb einer Konstruktion häufig Grenzen mit anderen Räumen unterschiedlicher Funktion teilen (beispielsweise können in einem Gebäude Büros, ein Hotel oder Wohnungen untergebracht sein). Manche Projekte belegen sogar genau diese Grenze – zum Beispiel Räume für den Internethandel. Funktionszentren und -zonen trennen das Büro in aufgabenorientierte Räume, die sich schnell an eine andere Funktion anpassen lassen (Just-in-time-Büro).

Die Entdeckung des „Humankapitals" bewirkte eine weitere Annäherung an den idealen Arbeitsplatz für Arbeitgeber und Arbeitnehmer. Das „Sick-Building"-Syndrom weckte bei Arbeitgebern allein aus wirtschaftlichen Gründen das Interesse an einer besseren Lebensqualität am Arbeitsplatz. Die Erkenntnis, dass zufällige Treffen in informellen Zonen, spontane Gespräche während der Arbeit und spontaner Wissensaustausch zu Kosteneinsparungen führen, sorgte für die Bereitstellung einer zwanglosen Arbeitsumgebung. Zugangsbereiche entwickelten sich von einem Kostenfaktor zu wertvollen kommunikativen Knotenpunkten für die Mitarbeiter. Ihren Aufenthalt dort unterstützen Wege und Brücken, die sich durch das Gebäude schlängeln. Der „Business Club" experimentiert mit einer neuen Anordnung. Hierbei schaffen kontrastierende Räume einschließlich Lounges eine Umgebung für alle Arbeitsabläufe und Zusammenkünfte einer hauptsächlich in Telearbeit beschäftigten Belegschaft.

*Masterpieces Office Architecture + Design* knüpft an den Erfolg der Publikation *Offices* an. Auch hier liegt der Schwerpunkt auf internationaler Büroarchitektur, allerdings unter dem neuen Blickwinkel des nachhaltigen, ökologischen Bauens.

prestige s'affirme de plus en plus – tant pour les immeubles abritant des entreprises privées que pour ceux des administrations et agences gouvernementales –, et qu'un même immeuble peut abriter non seulement des bureaux, mais aussi un hôtel ou des appartements. Certains bâtiments, notamment ceux des entreprises de commerce sur Internet, sont typiques de ce cas de figure. La tendance actuelle va vers une répartition de l'espace selon les tâches à effectuer, et vers la capacité des bureaux à s'adapter rapidement à de nouvelles fonctions (bureaux « juste-à-temps »).

D'autre part, la découverte de la valeur du capital humain pousse les architectes à optimiser les postes de travail au bénéfice tant de l'employeur que des employés. Il est clair que des immeubles malsains ne vont pas dans le sens de l'efficacité économique. Par delà cette évidence, on favorise maintenant les espaces propices aux réunions informelles et à l'échange spontané d'informations, qui contribuent à relaxer l'atmosphère de travail tout en réduisant les coûts. Quant au hall d'entrée, qui hier encore occasionnait des frais sans véritable contrepartie, c'est désormais un lieu de sociabilité, un véritable « club d'entreprise », un environnement propice aux réunions d'une équipe qui connaît la valeur de la communication interne.

Cet ouvrage s'inscrit dans la ligne du livre à succès de la publication *Offices*. Il présente des immeubles de bureaux construits dans le monde entier, qui mettent l'accent sur les nouvelles perspectives offertes par le développement durable et les technologies de construction écologiques.

PROJECTS. PRC

IEKTE. PROJETS.

# DELOITTE HEADQUARTERS,
## COPENHAGEN, DENMARK

# 3XN / KIM HERFORTH NIELSEN

www.3xn.com

**Client:** Deloitte Huset A/S, **Completion:** 2005, **Gross floor area:** 38,000 m², **Photos:** Adam Mørk.

Left: Exterior view by night. Links: Außenansicht bei Nacht. Gauche: Vue de nuit. | Right: Fourth floor plan. Rechts: Grundriss vierte Etage. Droite: Plan du 4e étage.

The three solitary buildings are located at the edge of land and water. Their openings, which prolong the outer perimeter, position all offices along the façades with panoramic views and fresh air access. The façades consist of double glass elements. The office areas and the central atrium form a single room with a large light installation at the bottom of the stairs. This supports an open and transparent business structure and informal knowledge sharing. The office areas are mostly designed as landscapes, with a number of back-up rooms such as study cells and meeting rooms also present at all levels.

Die drei Einzelgebäude sind am Ufer gelegen. Da die Fenster die Außenränder verlängern, können alle Büros entlang der Fassade liegen und Panoramaaussichten und frische Luft bieten. Die Fassaden bestehen aus einer Doppelverglasung. Bürobereiche und das zentrale Atrium bilden einen einzigen Raum mit einer großen Lichtinstallation an der Treppenunterseite. Dies unterstützt eine offene und transparente Unternehmensstruktur sowie einen informellen Wissensaustausch. Die Büros sind vorwiegend als Raumlandschaften gestaltet. Mehrere Back-Office-Bereiche wie Arbeitszellen und Besprechungsräume sind ebenfalls auf allen Ebenen vorhanden.

Ces trois immeubles distincts construits au bord de l'eau sont pourvus de ventilation naturelle et offrent des vues panoramiques sur les environs. Les façades se composent de double vitrage. Les bureaux sont dotés d'une décoration paysagère et ouverts sur la verrière centrale. Une grande installation lumineuse agrémente l'escalier. La transparence favorise la communication informelle entre les employés. Des espaces de travail individuels et des salles de réunion se trouvent à tous les étages.

Illuminated atrium. Beleuchtetes Atrium. Atrium illuminé.

From left to right, from above to below:
Workplaces, atrium, view into atrium.
Right: Informal meeting area.

Von links nach rechts, von oben nach unten:
Arbeitsplätze, Atrium, Blick ins Atrium.
Rechts: Informeller Treffpunkt.

De gauche à droite, de haut en bas:
Lieux de travail, atrium, vue sur l'atrium.
Droite: Point informel de rencontre.

# CONTEX HEADQUARTERS,
## SANTIAGO, CHILE

# 57STUDIO

www.57studio.com

**Client:** Empresa Constructora, **Completion:** 2004, **Gross floor area:** 1,600 m², **Photos:** Courtesy of 57Studio.

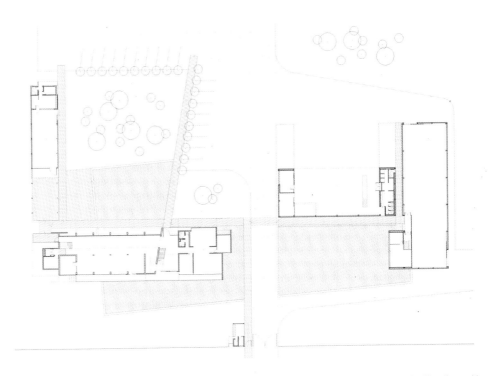

Left: Concrete façade. Links: Betonfassade. Gauche: Façade en béton. | Right: Floor plan. Rechts: Grundriss. Droite: Plan d'ensemble.

The assignment arises from a contest to build the dependencies of a construction company, with a diverse program of warehouse, workshop, offices and cafeteria. The proposal is based on taking the diversity of materials, the recognizable structures, and the basic shapes as architectonic elements that are present in the works of the company. The warehouse is characterized by the wavy plate and by its steel structure, while the workshop opens completely to the west, keeping equipment towards the edges. The offices stand out of being constructed of pure concrete with steel lattices, while the cafeteria appears as a glass pavilion.

Der Auftrag resultiert aus einem Wettbewerb für die Errichtung der Nebengebäude eines Bauunternehmens mit Lagerhaus, Werkhalle, Büros und Cafeteria. Der Bauplan sah vor, dass sich die Arbeit der Firma anhand einer Materialienvielfalt, wieder erkennbaren Konstruktionen und grundlegenden Formen präsentiert sowie einer Stahlkonstruktion, die das Lager kennzeichnet. Die zum Westen hin vollständig geöffnete Werkhalle enthält an den Rändern die Baustellenausrüstung. Die Konstruktion der Büros zeichnet sich durch den unbehandelten Beton mit Stahlgittern aus, während die Cafeteria als Glaspavillon erscheint.

L'objectif était ici de construire des locaux annexes pour une entreprise du BTP, notamment un entrepôt, un atelier, des bureaux et une cafétéria. Les architectes ont repris les divers matériaux et les formes de base utilisées dans les réalisations du client. L'entrepôt se caractérise par une structure en acier couverte par un toit ondulé. L'atelier s'ouvre entièrement sur le côté ouest. Les bureaux sont abrités par une structure en béton pourvue d'un treillis en acier. La cafétéria a été aménagée dans un pavillon en verre.

From left to right, from above to below:
Exterior detail, glazed façade,
wooden hallway, interior.
Right: Entrance view.

Von links nach rechts, von oben nach unten:
Detail Außenansicht, verglaste Fassade,
Außengang, Innenansicht.
Rechts: Eingangsansicht.

De gauche à droite, de haut en bas:
Détail de l'extérieur, façade vitrée,
couloir vers l'extérieur, intérieur.
Droite: Vue sur l'entrée.

# KP ALAZRAKI ADVERTISING AGENCY
## GUADALAJARA, MEXICO

# AD 11 SALVADOR MACIAS FRANCISCO GUTIERREZ

www.ad11.com.mx

Client: KP Alazraki, Completion: 2007, Gross floor area: 2,500 m², Photos: Mito Covarrubias.

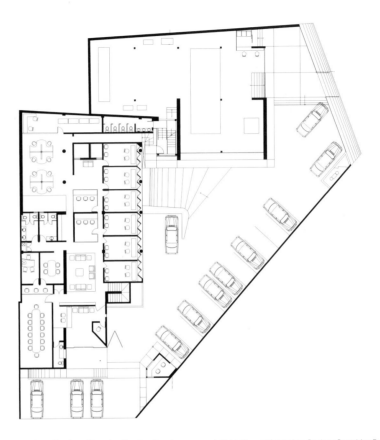

Left: Glazed façade. Links: Verglaste Fassade. Gauche: Façade en verre. | Right: Ground floor plan. Rechts: Grundriss Erdgeschoss. Droite: Plan du rez-de-chaussée.

The project consists of two buildings with different functions. One of them contains the administrative and creative offices, and the other one, the printing and production complex. The project's goal was to open up the façade in order to show what the company represents: a merchandising brand, and serve as an advertising billboard. The staircase acts as the communications articulator, maintaining the dialogue between the two buildings. To bring natural light into the working spaces was a fundamental part of the project, thus skylights were carefully placed to infuse the entire buildings with it.

Das Projekt umfasst zwei Gebäude mit unterschiedlichen Funktionen. Eines enthält die Verwaltungs- und Entwicklungsbüros, das andere den Druck- und Herstellungsbereich. Ziel des Projekts war eine Öffnung der Fassade, um das Unternehmen als Handelsmarke darzustellen und als Reklamefläche zu dienen. Das Treppenhaus funktioniert als Kommunikationsverbindung, um den Dialog zwischen den Mitarbeitern beider Gebäude zu pflegen. Ein Schwerpunkt liegt auf der natürlichen Belichtung der Arbeitsbereiche: Sorgfältig angeordnete Oberlichter erfüllen den gesamten Gebäudekomplex mit Licht.

Cet ensemble se compose de deux bâtiments remplissant des fonctions différentes. Le premier abrite les bureaux administratifs et ceux des créateurs, le second l'imprimerie et les installations de production. La tâche des architectes consistait à ouvrir la façade afin de symboliser l'ouverture d'esprit du client – une agence de publicité. Une cage d'escalier articule le dialogue entre les deux bâtiments. Le cahier des charges stipulant qu'une place importante devait être accordée à la lumière naturelle, les architectes ont conçu un éclairage zénithal qui se diffuse dans toutes les pièces.

From left to right, from above to below:
North façade of building 2,
north façade of building 1, lobby.
Right: Façade of building 1.

Von links nach rechts, von oben nach unten:
Nordfassade von Gebäude 2,
Nordfassade von Gebäude 1, Eingangshalle.
Rechts: Fassade von Gebäude 1.

De gauche à droite, de haut en bas:
Façade nord du bâtiment 2,
façade nord du bâtiment 1, hall d'entrée.
Droite: Façade du bâtiment 1.

# E.ON HEADQUARTERS
## MUNICH, GERMANY

# ADAM ARCHITEKTEN

www.adam-architekten.de

**Client:** E.ON Energie AG, **Completion:** 2008, **Gross floor area:** 9,000 m², **Photos:** Florian Schreiber, Munich.

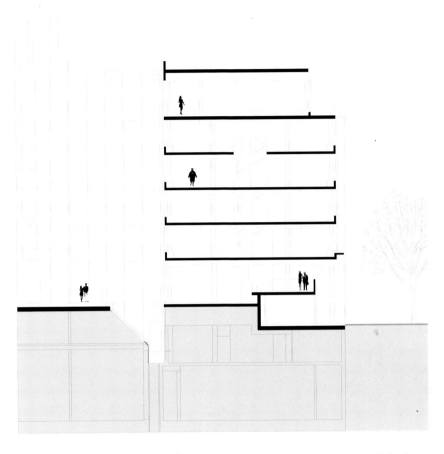

Left: Office floor. Links: Büroetage. Gauche: Étage des bureaux. | Right: Section. Rechts: Querschnitt. Droite: Coupe transversale.

With its ground floor canteen and several meeting rooms in the penthouse, the newly built corporate headquarters of E.ON Energie AG offers 120 combination offices on four floors. They are connected via three air spaces with spiral staircases. On the ground floor, the cafeteria is in part located on a deck extending across six meeting rooms. The staff lounge on the ground floor connects the glass-covered piazza with the new inner courtyard. Designed in cooperation with Dietmar Tanterl, building A's roof floor hallway connects the executive level with the supervisory board meeting room.

Mit der Kantine im Erdgeschoss und mehreren Besprechungsräumen im Penthouse bietet der Neubau der Konzernzentrale der E.ON Energie AG 120 Kombibüros in vier Geschossen. Sie sind über drei Lufträume mit Wendeltreppen verbunden. Im Erdgeschoss liegt das Casino zum Teil auf einem Deck, das über sechs Besprechungsräume gelegt wurde. Die Mitarbeiterlounge im Erdgeschoss des Hauses H verbindet die glasüberdeckte Piazza mit dem neuen Hof. Der in Zusammenarbeit mit Dietmar Tanterl gestaltete Flur im Dachgeschoss des Hauses A verbindet die Vorstandsebene mit dem Saal in dem der Aufsichtsrat tagt.

L'immeuble neuf qui abrite le siège social de la société E.ON Energie comprend une cantine au rez-de-chaussée, cent vingt bureaux répartis sur quatre étages reliés par trois grands escaliers en spirale, ainsi que des salles de réunion au niveau supérieur. La cantine a été aménagée sur une plate-forme couvrant six salles de réunion supplémentaires. Le foyer des employés, situé au rez-de-chaussée du bâtiment H, assure la liaison entre la grande verrière et la nouvelle cour. Le couloir du dernier étage de l'immeuble A, dont la décoration a été réalisée en collaboration avec Dietmar Tanterl, relie les bureaux de la direction avec la salle de réunion du conseil d'administration.

Staff lounge. Mitarbeiterlounge. Salon pour le personnel.

From left to right, from above to below:
Interior detail, cafeteria,
open working spaces, atrium.
Right: Hallway.

Von links nach rechts, von oben nach unten:
Detail Innenansicht, Kasino,
offene Arbeitsplätze, Atrium.
Rechts: Flur.

De gauche à droite, de haut en bas:
Détail de l'intérieur, cafétéria,
espaces de travail, atrium.
Droite: Couloir.

# COCOON
## ZURICH, SWITZERLAND

# CAMENZIND EVOLUTION

www.camenzindevolution.com
**Client:** Swiss Life, Zurich, **Completion:** 2007, **Gross floor area:** 1,900 m², **Photos:** Camenzind Evolution,
Romeo Gross (32, 33), Ferit Kuyas (30, 34 b.r., 35).

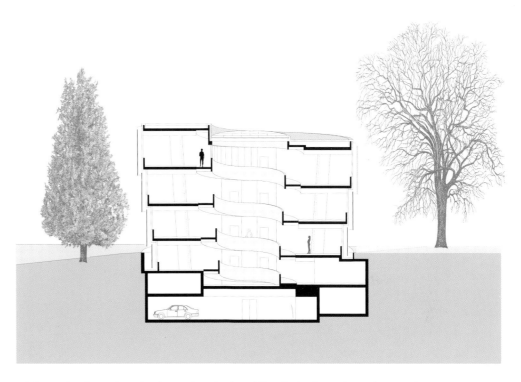

Left: **Exterior view.** Links: **Außenansicht.** Gauche: Vue de l'extérieur. | Right: **Section.** Rechts: **Querschnitt.** Droite: Coupe transversale.

The distinctive solitary building is the result of a novel concept of internal spatial connections that interact with the environment. A variety of work and use concepts emerged from the omission of the classic horizontal arrangement of floors. All spaces are arranged helically along a gently inclined access and communication ramp and surround a light-flooded atrium. The delicate stainless-steel mesh wire of the façade veils the sculpture-like building during the day and allows it to shine as an illuminated, transparent shape during the night.

Der markante Solitärbau ist das Ergebnis einer neuartigen Konzeption von internen räumlichen Beziehungen im Zusammenspiel mit der Umgebung. Indem auf die Anordnung klassischer horizontaler Geschosse verzichtet wurde, ergeben sich vielfältige Arbeits- und Nutzungskonzepte. Sämtliche Flächen sind spiralförmig entlang einer sanft ansteigenden Erschließungs- und Kommunikationsrampe angeordnet und umgeben ein lichtdurchflutetes Atrium. Das feine Edelstahl-Drahtgeflecht der Fassade verhüllt tagsüber das skulpturartige Gebäude und lässt es nachts als leuchtenden, transparenten Körper scheinen.

Cet immeuble qui ne passe pas inaperçu est le résultat d'une nouvelle conception des rapports entre les espaces intérieurs et l'environnement d'un bâtiment. Les architectes ont ici renoncé aux étages horizontaux classiques, rendant ainsi possible une multitude de concepts d'utilisation. Tous les espaces intérieurs sont desservis par une spirale en pente douce qui se déroule autour d'une verrière centrale. Le fin treillis en acier inox qui couvre la façade filtre la lumière du jour et donne au bâtiment un aspect lumineux et transparent la nuit.

Working spaces. Arbeitsplätze. Espace de travail.

From left to right, from above to below:
Atrium, lobby,
conference room, glazed ceiling.
Right: Lounge.

Von links nach rechts, von oben nach unten:
Atrium, Eingangshalle,
Besprechungsraum, verglaster Dachhimmel.
Rechts: Lounge.

De gauche à droite, de haut en bas:
Atrium, hall d'entrée,
salle de conférence, verrière.
Droite: Coin salon.

# GOOGLE EMEA ENGINEERING HUB
## ZURICH, SWITZERLAND

# CAMENZIND EVOLUTION

www.camenzindevolution.com

**Client:** Google Inc., **Completion:** 2008, **Gross floor area:** 12,000 m², **Photos:** Peter Wurmli.

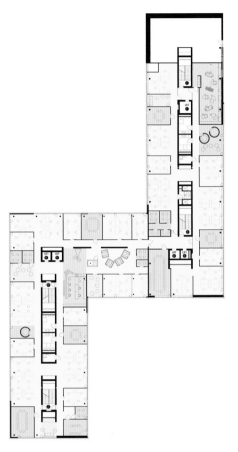

Left: Reception. Links: Empfang. Gauche: Réception. | Right: Second floor plan. Rechts: Grundriss 2. Etage. Droite: Plan du 2e étage.

Google's new EMEA Engineering Hub cultivates an energized and inspiring work environment that is relaxed but focused, and buzzing with activities. The new Google office is about functionality and flexibility in the personal workspace, and choice and diversity in the community areas, creating an environment that holistically supports the Googlers in their work and well-being. The research undertaken by the architects extended beyond purely functional aspects, and provided information about the Googlers personality types, representational systems, values and motivational factors.

Die Arbeitsumgebung von Googles neuem Technikzentrum für Europa, den Nahen Osten und Afrika verleiht Energie, stimuliert, ist zwanglos, doch konzentriert und von geschäftigem Treiben geprägt. In den Büros sind die persönlichen Arbeitsbereiche auf Funktionalität und Flexibilität ausgerichtet. Die Gemeinschaftsbereiche bieten hierzu Alternativen mit vielfältiger Gestaltung. Das so geschaffene Umfeld fördert ganzheitlich die Arbeit und das Wohlempfinden der „Googler". Die Studien der Architekten liefern neben funktionalen Aspekten auch Erkenntnisse über Persönlichkeitstypen, Repräsentationssysteme, Wertvorstellungen und Motivationsfaktoren.

Les nouveaux locaux techniques de Google se caractérisent par une atmosphère à la fois détendue et dynamique. Afin de favoriser la productivité et le bien-être des employés, les espaces de travail personnalisés mettent l'accent sur la fonctionnalité et la flexibilité, tandis que les espaces communs privilégient le choix et la diversité. Les recherches menées par les architectes ont dépassé l'aspect purement fonctionnel, pour aborder des thèmes aussi variés que la personnalité des employés, les différents systèmes de valeurs au sein de l'entreprise et les facteurs de motivation au travail.

Terrace

Please close
door!

Informal meeting space. Informeller Besprechungsraum. Point de rencontre.

From left to right, from above to below:
Meeting area, office,
meeting igloo, restaurant with slide.
Right: Meeting spaces.

Von links nach rechts, von oben nach unten:
Besprechungszimmer, Büro,
Iglu, Restaurant mit Rutsche.
Rechts: Besprechungsräume.

De gauche à droite, de haut en bas:
Salle de rencontre, bureau,
salle de réunion igloo, restaurant avec toboggan.
Droite: Salles de réunion.

# CHATEAU CRENEAU INTERNATIONAL HEADOFFICE
## HASSELT, BELGIUM

# CHATEAU CRENEAU INTERNATIONAL

www.creneau.com

**Client:** Creneau International nv, **Completion:** 2004, **Gross floor area:** 1,160 m², **Photos:** Philippe van Gelooven.

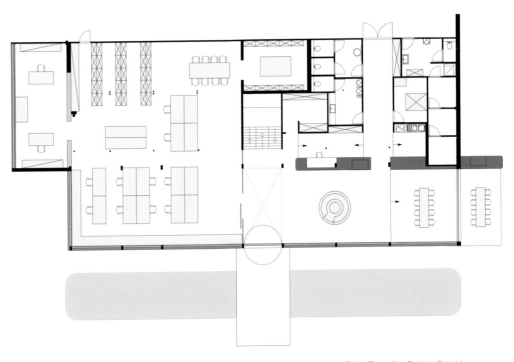

Left: Landscaped office. Links: Bürolandschaft. Gauche: Architecture intérieure des bureaux. | Right: Floor plan. Rechts: Grundriss. Droite: Plan d'ensemble.

It is obvious that design is Creneau's core business. The ground floor design department overlooks the hallway via a glass wall. The hall is shady and tranquil, contrasting with the fresh, active and bright concept of the design area. Unconventionally, the hallway serves as both a dining and a meeting room. Visitors may arrive amid the homely impression of a busy lunch break. Carpeting, wallpaper and soft colors create a serene atmosphere on the first floor. Typically for Creneau, the Château concept is a fascinating mixture of styles and atmospheres. The ideal home for the "Atmosphere Architects!"

Es ist offensichtlich, dass Innenarchitektur das Kerngeschäft von Creneau ausmacht. Im Erdgeschoss blickt die Designabteilung durch eine Glaswand über den Flur. Das frische, aktive und helle Konzept des Designbereichs kontrastiert mit der dunkleren und ruhigen Halle. Auf unkonventionelle Weise dient die Halle gleichzeitig als Ess- und Besprechungszimmer. Besucher können mitunter die häusliche Atmosphäre eines geschäftigen Mittagessens erleben. Im ersten Obergeschoss erzeugen Teppichböden, Tapeten und gedämpfte Farben eine friedliche Atmosphäre. Wie für Creneau typisch, ist das Château-Konzept eine faszinierende Mischung aus Stilen und Stimmungen.

Ce bâtiment a été conçu pour une entreprise de design. Le rez-de-chaussée donne sur un hall situé en contrebas grâce à une paroi en verre. L'aspect tranquille et sombre du hall d'entrée contraste avec l'agitation et la clarté des bureaux. Ce hall a reçu une affectation inhabituelle, puisqu'il sert à la fois de réfectoire et de salle de réunion. Au premier étage, la moquette, le papier peint et des couleurs douces créent une atmosphère de sérénité. Le concept « Château », typique des créations du client, se compose d'un mélange de styles impressionnant. Bref, ces locaux sont l'idéal pour Creneau International, les « architectes de l'atmosphère ».

From left to right, from above to below:
Lobby with glass chandelier, diner and meeting room,
exterior with picnic tables, conference room.
Right: Working space.

Von links nach rechts, von oben nach unten:
Empfangshalle mit Glaskronleuchter, Ess- und Besprechungszimmer,
Außenansicht mit Picknicktischen, Konferenzraum.
Rechts: Arbeitsplätze.

De gauche à droite, de haut en bas:
Hall d'accueil avec chandelier, salle de réception et de dîner,
vue de l'extérieur avec tables de pic-nic, salle de conférence.
Droite: Espace de travail.

**GREY WORLDWIDE**
HAMBURG, GERMANY

## COSSMANN_DE BRUYN
## ARCHITECTURE INTERIOR DESIGN

www.cossmann-debruyn.de
**Client:** GREY Worldwide Deutschland GmbH, **Completion:** 2005, **Gross floor area:** 3,060 m², **Photos:**
Bernd Haugrund, ArtDoku.

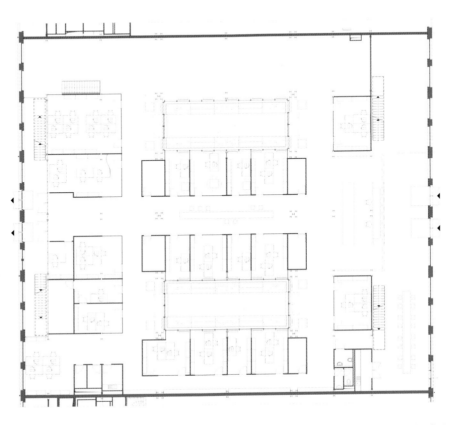

Left: Counter in lobby. Links: Theke in Empfangshalle. Gauche: Hall d'accueil avec comptoir. | Right: Ground floor plan. Rechts: Grundriss Erdgeschoss. Droite: Plan du rez-de-chaussée.

For the advertising agency GREY Worldwide a listed hall of the former tram depot was converted to a working ambience with loft quality for approximately 120 employees consisting of four different communication disciplines. The design and completion of the interior support openness and transparency between single and open-plan offices, between workplaces and inlying, glazed atria as well as between lounges and representation areas creating a motivating working environment. By means of powerful and surprising details, a selection of materials that intensify the building character and utilising the colors of the corporate design a vitalising and inspiring atmosphere was created.

Für die Werbeagentur GREY Worldwide wurde eine denkmalgeschützte Halle des ehemaligen Straßenbahndepots in ein Arbeitsambiente mit Loftqualität für circa 120 Mitarbeiter aus vier verschiedenen Kommunikationsdisziplinen umgestaltet. Das Interieur impliziert Offenheit und Transparenz zwischen Einzelbüros und Bürolandschaften, Arbeitsplätzen und verglasten Atrien sowie Aufenthalts- und Repräsentationsbereichen, so schaffen sie eine motivierende Arbeitswelt. Durch kraftvolle und überraschende Details, die Auswahl der Materialien, die den Gebäudecharakter verstärken und den Einsatz der Farben des Corporate Design entsteht eine lebendige, inspirierende Atmosphäre.

L'agence de publicité internationale Grey s'est installée dans un ancien dépôt de tramway classé monument historique. Environ cent vingt employés de quatre disciplines différentes du domaine de la communication travaillent dans ce loft. Les aménagements intérieurs mettent l'accent sur la transparence et l'ouverture dans les bureaux individuels, la verrière, le foyer et les zones de convivialité, créant ainsi un environnement de travail motivant. L'atmosphère vivifiante de ce loft vient de l'intégration de détails surprenants, d'un choix de matériaux visant à mettre en relief le caractère du bâtiment, et de l'utilisation de couleurs issues du visuel d'entreprise Grey.

From left to right, from above to below:
Lobby with conference area at first floor,
bar in lobby with meeting point, office area.
Right: Metting point.

Von links nach rechts, von oben nach unten:
Empfangshalle mit Besprechungsraum in der ersten Etage,
Empfangstheke mit Meetingpoint, Bürobereiche.
Right: Meetingpoint.

De gauche à droite, de haut en bas:
Point de rencontre au 1er étage,
hall d'entrée, espace de travail.
Droite: Salle d'accueil.

# A.T. KEARNEY

## DÜSSELDORF, GERMANY

www.cossmann-debruyn.de
Client: A.T. Kerney GmbH, Completion: 2004, Gross floor area: 3,816 m², Photos: Nicole Zimmermann.

Left: Illuminated installations. Links: Beleuchtete Einrichtungen. Gauche: Espace avec installations lumineuses. | Right: Floor plans. Rechts: Grundrisse. Droite: Plans d'ensemble.

The colors of the wall and ceiling range from white to aquamarine in harmony with the glass walls of the hall. In the conference and back office area on the ground floor, the aquamarine takes backstage to a white to sandy color spectrum, matching the oak parquet. High-tech fabric wall and furniture covers contrast with the smoother surface of the office walls, creating an acoustically, visually and physically appealing effect. A straight interior design concept, harmonized lighting, and uniform highly functional office furniture, individualized for A. T. Kearney, support the crispness and integrity.

Die lichten Wand- und Deckenfarben harmonieren in ihrer Skala von weiß bis aquamarin mit den Glaswänden des Flures. Der Konferenz- und Bürobereich im Erdgeschoss ist passend zum Eichenparkett weiß bis sandfarben gehalten. Möbelbezüge und Wandverkleidungen aus hochmodernem Gewebe bilden einen Kontrast zu den glatten Oberflächen der Bürowände; dies verbessert die Akustik und erzeugt einen optisch und haptisch angenehmen Reiz. Die Beleuchtung ist ebenso auf das geradlinige und frische Gestaltungskonzept abgestimmt wie das hochfunktionale Büromöbelprogramm, das für A.T. Kearney individualisiert wurde.

La couleur des murs et plafonds varie du blanc au bleu marine et s'harmonise aux parois en verre du hall d'entrée. Dans la salle de conférence et la zone de gestion situées au rez-de-chaussée, le bleu cède la place à des tons blancs et sable en harmonie avec la teinte du parquet en chêne. Le tissu high-tech qui couvre les murs et les meubles contraste avec les surfaces plus tendres qui donnent aux bureaux un aspect accueillant. Une ambiance tonifiante se dégage de la décoration intérieure, caractérisée par un éclairage harmonisé et un mobilier de bureau à la fois personnalisé et hautement fonctionnel.

From left to right, from above to below:
Lounge in lobby, lounge at meeting point,
meeting point, recreation room.
Right: Meeting point.

Von links nach rechts, von oben nach unten:
Lounge-Empfang, Lounge-Meetingpoint,
Meetingpoint, Boardingroom.
Rechts: Meetingpoint.

De gauche à droite, de haut en bas:
Coin salon, point informel de rencontre,
point de ralliement, salle de conférence.
Droite: Cafétéria.

# OFFICE AND PRESENTATION BUILDING
# TERMINAL V
## LAUTERACH, AUSTRIA

# HUGO DWORZAK

www.austria-architets.com/architekturwerkstatt_dworzak
**Client:** Hefel Wohnbau AG, **Completion:** 2000, **Gross floor area:** 1,800 m², **Photos:** Craig Kuhner, Günther Laznia.

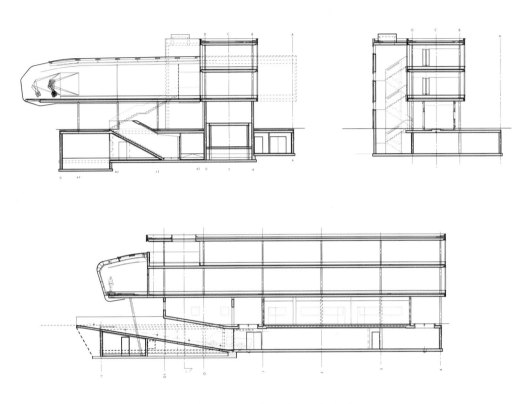

Left: Staircase. Links: Aufgang. Gauche: Escalier. | Right: Sections. Rechts: Schnitte. Droite: Coupes.

The company located in a residential building not only wanted to expand its office space but, more importantly, needed a multimedia presentation room for 3D animations of their structural projects. The room, where the presentation of the non-contextual "No place" could be viewed, is a middle ground between reality and virtual space. Already when entering this connecting space, a transferal of the architectural medium from reality into simulated reality should occur. The multi-leaf wall structure, displaced in relation to itself makes possible the indirect addition of natural or artificial light and with it, adjustable amounts of reality alteration.

Das in einem Wohngebäude ansässige Unternehmen wünschte nicht nur die Erweiterung seiner Bürofläche. Entscheidender war sein Bedarf an einem multimedialen Präsentationsraum für die 3-D-Animationen seiner Wohnbauprojekte. Der Raum, in dem der kontextlose „Nichtort" präsentiert werden könnte, ist ein Zwischenraum von Realität und Virtualität. Bereits beim Betreten dieser räumlichen Verbindung sollte über das Medium Architektur ein Transfer von der Realität zur simulierten Realität stattfinden. Der mehrschalige, zueinander versetzte Wandaufbau ermöglicht die indirekte Führung von natürlichem oder künstlichem Licht und damit regelbare Mengen an Veränderungen der Realität.

Une entreprise installée dans un immeuble résidentiel souhaitait agrandir ses locaux et surtout disposer d'une salle multimédia pour présenter ses animations 3D. L'espace de visualisation que les architectes ont réalisé est à mi-chemin entre réalité et virtualité dans la mesure où l'on passe de l'une à l'autre dès qu'on accède au vestibule. L'enveloppe multicouches aux formes futuristes permet de doser la lumière naturelle et artificielle de manière à modifier l'apparence de la réalité.

Interior presentation space. Innenansicht Präsentationsraum. Intérieur de la salle de réunion.

From left to right, from above to below:
Exterior north façade, south façade,
connecting tunnel, east façade.
Right: Interior 3D presentation space.

Von links nach rechts, von oben nach unten:
Außenansicht Nordfassade, Südfassade,
Verbindungstunnel, Ostfassade.
Rechts: Innenansicht 3D Präsentationszentrum.

De gauche à droite, de haut en bas:
Façade nord vue de l'extérieur, façade sud,
tunnel reliant, façade est.
Droite: Vue intérieure sur la salle de présentation en 3D.

# VAN DER LAAT & JIMÉNEZ HEADQUARTERS,
## SAN JOSÉ, COSTA RICA

# FORO ARQUITECTOS / FOURNIER-ROJAS ARQUITECTOS

www.foroarq.net
Client: Construction Company Van der Laat & Jiménez, Completion: 2005, Gross floor area: 2,300 m²,
Photos: Rodrigo Montoya.

Left: Circular stairs. Links: Kreisförmige Treppe. Gauche: Escalier en colimaçon. | Right: Second floor plan. Rechts: Grundriss 2. Etage.
Droite: Plan du 2e étage.

The program of the building demanded new office headquarters for V & J, one of Costa Rica's oldest and most important construction firms. A new 3-story addition and the remodeling of an existing 2-story building were undertaken by the architects. The exterior is executed using concrete tiles and pre-painted copper sheathing on structural reinforced concrete and features enameled painted steel-plate windows. Enclosed parking occupies the ground level, while the upper levels are office space.

Das Programm beinhaltete eine neue Bürozentrale für V & J, eines der ältesten und bedeutendsten Bau-unternehmen Costa Ricas. Die Architekten realisier-ten einen dreigeschossigen Anbau und den Umbau eines zweigeschossigen Gebäudes. Die Außenwand wurde mit Betonfliesen und einer grundierten Kup-ferverkleidung auf Stahlbeton überzogen, außerdem wurden lackierte Stahlblechfenster eingefügt. Im Erdgeschoss befinden sich Parkplätze, während die oberen Geschosse Büroflächen beherbergen.

Cet édifice abrite le siège social d'une des plus anciennes et plus importantes entreprises de BTP du Costa Rica. Les architectes ont modernisé un immeuble de deux étages préexistant et construit un nouveau bâtiment de trois étages. Une structure en béton armé supporte des plaques en béton et un re-vêtement en cuivre. Elle s'ouvre par des fenêtres en acier émaillé. Les bureaux sont installés au-dessus du parking aménagé au rez-de-chaussée.

From left to right, from above to below:
Exterior view, façade of concrete tiles,
office space, skylight.
Right: Interior.

Von links nach rechts, von oben nach unten:
Außenansicht, Betonfassade,
Büroräume, Oberlicht.
Rechts: Innenansicht.

De gauche à droite, de haut en bas:
Vue de l'extérieur, façade en béton,
bureau de travail, lucarne.
Droite: Vue de l'intérieur.

# 3ALITY DIGITAL,
## BURBANK, CA, USA

# FUNG + BLATT ARCHITECTS, INC.

www.fungandblatt.com

**Client:** Steve Schlair, **Completion:** 2007, **Gross floor area:** 1,860 m², **Photos:** Deborah Bird.

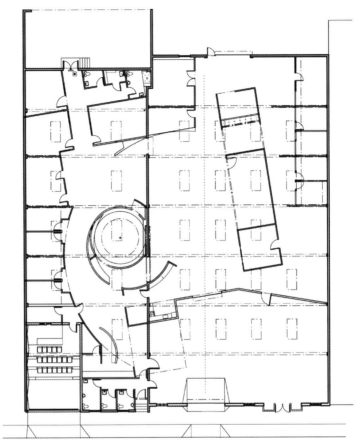

Left: Meeting area. Links: Aufenthaltsraum. Gauche: Point de rencontre. | Right: Floor plan. Rechts: Grundriss. Droite: Plan d'ensemble.

This digital film production facility inhabits two bays of an industrial building from the 1940s, separated by a bearing wall that allowed very limited open passage between the spaces. The architects were charged with designing a dynamic work environment with administrative and technical wings that include offices, workshops, editing rooms, equipment cage, screening room and long sight lines for camera staging. They introduced a circular conference room that becomes the vortex of the environment. It straddles the central dividing wall and propels into motion a series of ripples whose trajectories penetrate and diminish the wall separation, while establishing auxiliary spaces for informal gathering.

Die digitale Filmproduktionsfirma belegt zwei Hallen eines Fabrikgebäudes aus den 1940er Jahren. Da sie eine tragende Wand trennte, war zwischen den Bereichen nur ein sehr begrenzter Durchgang möglich. Die Architekten sollten eine dynamische Arbeitsumgebung mit Trakten für Verwaltung und Technik schaffen. Hierzu integrierten sie ein rundes Besprechungszimmer, das zum Dreh- und Angelpunkt des Arbeitsplatzes wird. Es spreizt die mittlere Trennwand und setzt eine Reihe von Wellen in Bewegung, deren Verlauf die Wand durchdringt und ihre trennende Wirkung verringert, während sie Nebenräume für informelle Treffen bereitstellt.

Une société de production de films numériques est installée dans un immeuble industriel construit dans les années 1940. Les locaux sont partagés par un mur porteur où de petites ouvertures permettent une communication restreinte entre les deux entités. La tâche des architectes consistait à créer un environnement de travail dynamique composé de bureaux, d'ateliers, de salles de mixage, de locaux techniques et d'une salle de projection. Une salle de conférence circulaire forme l'élément clé du concept retenu. Aménagée de part et d'autre du mur central, elle inclut divers cloisonnements ondulés qui structurent l'espace en créant des zones de regroupement annexes de manière à limiter l'effet de barrage du mur principal.

From left to right, from above to below:
Entry conference room, bearing wall, lobby.
Right: View into circular conference room.

Von links nach rechts, von oben nach unten:
Eingang zum Konferenzraum, tragende Wand, Eingangshalle.
Rechts: Blick in den kreisrunden Konferenzraum.

De gauche à droite, de haut en bas:
Entrée de la salle de conférence, mur porteur, hall d'accueil.
Droite: Vue sur la salle de conférence circulaire.

# KÖLNTRIANGLE,
## COLOGNE, GERMANY

310 BAUBEGINN DER ERSTEN RHEINBRUECKE UNTER KAISER KONSTANTIN UND DES KASTELLS DIVITIA, WORAUS DER NAME DEUTZ ENTSTEHT. NACH 430 WIRD DAS KASTELL DURCH FRAENKISCHE EROBERER ZUM KOENIGSHOF, ALS NAME BELEGT: DIVITIA CIVITAS. UM 1002-03 GRUENDET ERZBISCHOF HERIBERT AM RHEINUFER EIN BENEDIKTINERKLOSTER, UM 1020 WEIHE DER ABTEIKIRCHE ST. HERIBERT. 1230 DEUTZ WIRD ALS STADT BEZEICHNET UND FUEHRT EIN STADTSIEGEL. SEIT DEM SPAETMITTELALTER ZAHLREICHE ZERSTOERUNGEN DER STADT DEUTZ. NACH 1815 BAUEN DIE PREUSSEN DEUTZ UND KOELN ZUR STAERKSTEN FESTUNG IM WESTEN AUS, DEUTZ WIRD PREUSSISCHE GARNISONSSTADT. 1847 EROEFFNUNG DER GESAMTSTRECKE DER KOELN-MINDENER-EISENBAHN VON DEUTZ NACH MINDEN MIT BAHNHOF AN DIESER STELLE. 1859 UNTER KOENIG FRIEDERICH WILHELM IV. ROLLT DER ERSTE ZUG UEBER DIE ERSTE FESTE RHEINBRUECKE SEIT DER ROEMERZEIT. 1864 WIRD IN KOELN DIE ERSTE MOTORENFABRIK DER WELT GEGRUENDET, DIE SEIT 1872 ALS "GASMOTORENFABRIK DEUTZ" FIRMIERTE. 1888 DEUTZ WIRD DURCH EINGEMEINDUNG STADTTEIL VON KOELN. 1913 KUPPELBAU DES DEUTZER BAHNHOFS. DER BAHNHOFSVORPLATZ IST NACH DEM ERFINDER DES GASBETRIEBENEN VERBRENNUNGSMOTORS NICOLAUS AUGUST OTTO BENANNT. 1924 GRUENDUNG DER KOELNER MESSE UNTER OBERBUERGERMEISTER KONRAD ADENAUER. 1936 EROEFFNUNG DES RHEINISCHEN MUSEUMS IN DER EHEMALIGEN KUERASSIERKASERNE DEUTZ ALS "HAUS DER RHEINISCHEN HEIMAT". 1957 DER DEUTZER RHEINPARK WIRD STANDORT DER ERSTEN BUNDESGARTENSCHAU. 1959 EINWEIHUNG DES LANDESHAUSES IN DEUTZ ALS SITZ DES LANDSCHAFTSVERBANDES RHEINLAND. 1998 BAU DER KOELNARENA UND DES STADTHAUSES. 2006 EROEFFNUNG DER NEUEN MESSE HALLEN UND KOELN TRIANGLE.

# GATERMANN + SCHOSSIG

www.gatermann-schossig.de

**Client:** Rheinische Versorgungskassen, **Completion:** 2006, **Gross floor area:** 84,300 m², **Photos:** Jens Willebrand, Cologne (68, 70, 71, 72 a.r., 72 b.l., 72 b.r., 73), Gatermann + Schossig (72 a.l.).

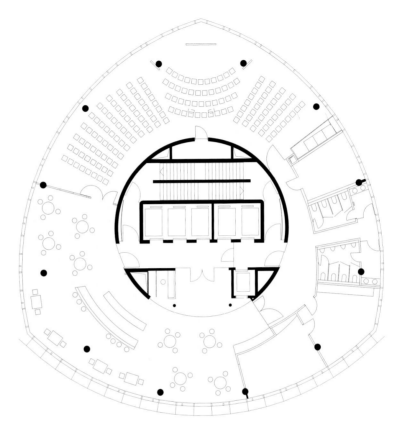

Left: Entrance hall. Links: Eingangshalle. Gauche: Hall d'entrée. | Right: Event floor plan. Rechts: Grundriss vom Veranstaltungsgeschoss. Droite: Plan de l'étage des manifestations.

With three convex element façades, the Cologne Triangle is defined by its Reuleaux form. In combination with the round center of the building, the ground plan resembling a Wankel engine results in spaces of varying depth, allowing the creation of a range of office sizes.

An innovative, decentralized energy concept offers floor-by-floor flexibility. The ventilated double façade provides optimal sun protection without blocking the view from within. Two dampers integrated into the façade ensure additional temperature control and fresh air ventilation.

Mit den drei konvex gebogenen Elementfassaden wird das KölnTriangel durch seine Reuleaux-Form geprägt. Sein Grundriss ähnelt einem Wankelmotor und ergibt in Verbindung mit dem runden Kern des Gebäudes unterschiedliche Raumtiefen, die eine variable Gestaltung der Büroflächen gestatten. Ein innovatives dezentrales Energiekonzept gewährleistet geschossweise Flexibilität. Die hinterlüftete Doppelfassade bietet optimalen Sonnenschutz ohne Beeinträchtigung der Aussicht. Für zusätzlichen Komfortgewinn und Frischluftzufuhr sorgen zwei fassadenintegrierte Kiemenfenster.

Trois façades convexes donnent à ce bâtiment un plan en forme de triangle de Reuleaux. L'espace central circulaire confère par ailleurs à l'ensemble l'aspect d'un piston de moteur rotatif. Avec pour résultat des espaces intérieurs de profondeur variable où il est possible d'aménager des bureaux de tailles différentes. Un concept énergétique innovant et décentralisé accroît encore la flexibilité interne. La double façade ventilée offre une protection optimale face au rayonnement solaire et offre des vues panoramiques sur l'extérieur. Deux dispositifs d'humidification de l'air intégrés à la façade contribuent également à la régulation thermique du bâtiment.

European Aviation Safety Agency

Agence Européenne de la Sécurité Aérienne

Europäische Agentur für Flugsicherheit

RHEINOR...
ERSTE MOTOREN...
ALS "GASMOTORENFABRI...
DURCH EINGEMEINDUNG STADT...
DES DEUTZER BAHNHOFS. DE...
DEM ERFINDER DES GASBETR...
NICOLAUS AUGUST OTTO BE...
KOELNER MESSE UNTER O...
ADENAUER. 1936 EROEFFNUM...
DER EHEMALIGEN KUERAS...
DER RHEINISCHEN HEIMAT".
STANDORT DER ERS...
1959 EINWEIHUNG DES LAND...
LANDSCHAFTSVERBAND...
KOELNARENA UND DES...
DER NEUEN...
MESSEHAL...

Entrance hall. Eingangshalle. Hall d'entrée.

From left to right, from above to below:
Double façade to the south, lobby,
office spaces, elevators.
Right: Office space.

Von links nach rechts, von oben nach unten:
Doppelte Südfassade, Empfangsraum,
Büros, Fahrstühle.
Rechts: Büros.

De gauche à droite, de haut en bas:
Double façade orientation sud,
hall d'accueil, bureaux, ascenseurs.
Droite: Bureaux.

# CAPRICORNHAUS DÜSSELDORF,
## DÜSSELDORF, GERMANY

# GATERMANN + SCHOSSIG

www.gatermann-schossig.de
**Client:** Capricorn Development GmbH & Co. KG, **Completion:** 2006, **Gross floor area:** 43,000 m², **Photos:** Rainer Rehfeld, Cologne (74), Gatermann + Schossig (76-77, 78).

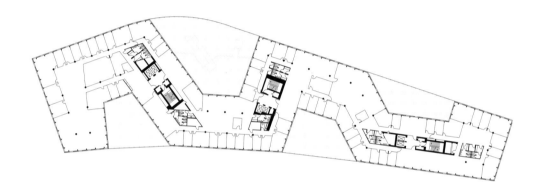

Left: Red glass panels façade. Fassade aus roten Glaspaneelen. Gauche: Façade de panneaux vitrés rouges. | Right: Typical floor plan. Rechts: Regelgeschoss Droite: Plan caractéristique de l'ensemble.

The unique new building with its red glass paneling is distinguished by its i-module façade. The location of the building, which is subject to a large degree of noise pollution, led to the design of a multifunctional façade module containing the entire individual room climate control technology. The façade features a ventilation system for cooling, heating and heat recovery, in addition to lighting, noise absorption, and room acoustics elements. The elimination of conventional building technology areas by the decentralized concept provided the interior planning with a great degree of freedom.

Die Besonderheit des prägnanten Neubaus mit seinen roten Glaspaneelen liegt vor allem in der erdachten i-modul Fassade. Die schallemissionsbelastete Lage des Gebäudes führte zur Entwicklung des multifunktionalen Fassadenmodules, das die gesamte notwendige Technik, um das individuelle Raumklima zu steuern, beinhaltet. Es ist ausgestattet mit einem eigenen Lüftungssystem zum Kühlen, Heizen, Lüften und zur Wärmerückgewinnung. Außerdem sind in dem Fassadenpaneel Beleuchtungs-, Schallabsorption- und Raumakkustikelemente integriert. Der Wegfall traditioneller Technikflächen durch das dezentrale Konzept bringt große Freiheitsgrade bei der inneren Gebäudeplanung mit sich.

Ce bâtiment étant construit dans une zone bruyante, il a été nécessaire d'élaborer un module de façade multifonctionnel qui intègre non seulement un système d'isolation acoustique, mais aussi des éléments d'éclairage et tout le dispositif de climatisation (refroidissement, chauffage, ventilation et récupération de chaleur). Les locaux techniques traditionnels étant ainsi superflus, les aménagements intérieurs ont pu être réalisés très librement.

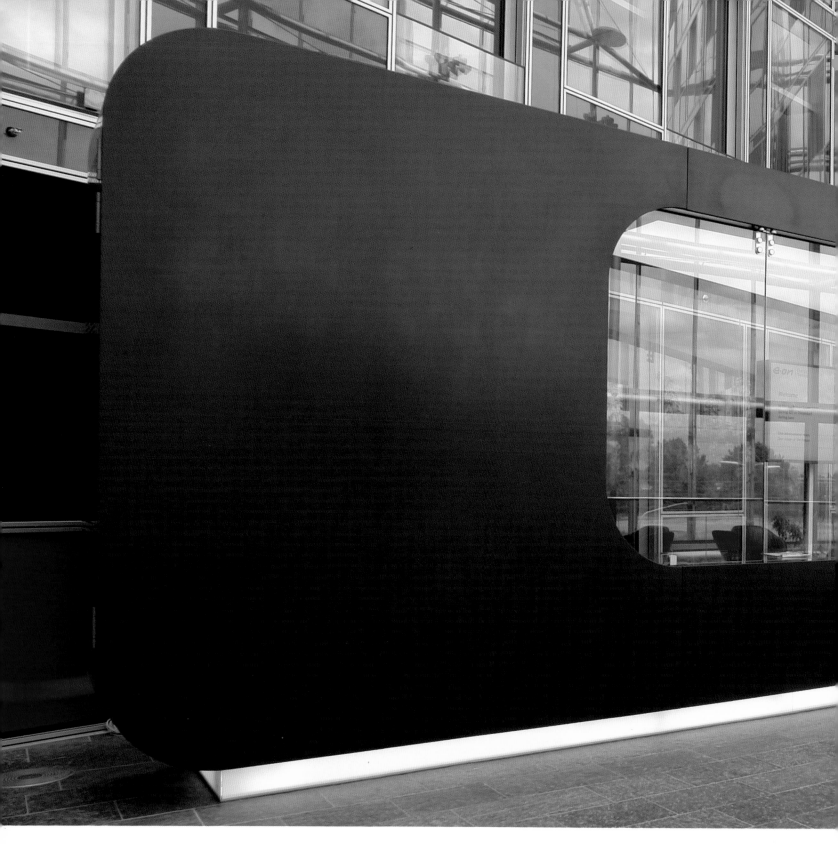

Entrance hall. Empfangshalle. Hall d'accueil.

From left to right, from above to below:
Cafeteria, open office spaces,
informal meeting area, interior.
Right: Detail façade.

Von links nach rechts, von oben nach unten:
Kasino, Bürolandschaft,
informeller Treffpunkt, Inneneinrichtung.
Rechts: Fassadendetail.

De gauche à droite, de haut en bas:
Cafétéria, espaces de travail,
point informel de rencontre, intérieur.
Droite: Détail de la façade.

**111 SOUTH WACKER,**
CHICAGO, IL, USA

# GOETTSCH PARTNERS

www.gpchicago.com
**Client:** The John Buck Company, **Completion:** 2005, **Gross floor area:** 135,360 m², **Photos:** James Steinkamp, Steinkamp Photography.

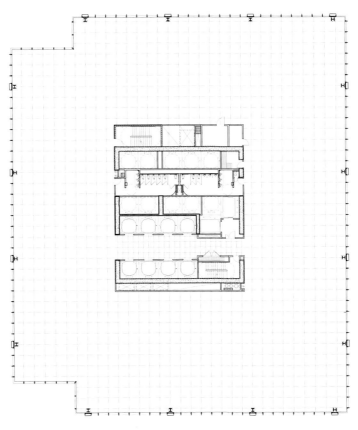

Left: Exterior west façade. Links: Außenansicht Westfassade. Gauche: Façade extérieure ouest. | Right: Typical floor plan. Rechts: Regelgeschossplan. Droite: Plan caractéristique.

Typical office floors are entirely column-free, to allow for planning efficiency and flexibility. The building's lobby is one of its more unique features, with a spiraling parking ramp that defines the space. The radial pattern of the ramp is reflected in the lobby's stepped ceiling, and this pattern is further echoed in the granite and marble floor that extends beyond the enclosure. Wrapping the lobby is a cable-supported, ultra-transparent glass wall that allows inside and outside to be perceived as a single, continuous space.

Die Regelgeschosse für Büros sind zugunsten von Planungseffizienz und -flexibilität gänzlich stützenfrei. Die Lobby des Gebäudes mit ihrer spiralförmigen, den Raum bestimmenden Parkrampe gehört zu den unverwechselbaren Charakteristika. Das radiale Muster der Rampe spiegelt sich in der abgestuften Decke der Lobby wider. Außerdem wird es vom Granit- und Marmorboden aufgegriffen, der sich auch außerhalb der Umbauung fortsetzt. Die Lobby ist von einer seilgestützten hochtransparenten Glaswand umgeben, wodurch innen und außen wie ein durchgehender Raum erscheinen.

La tendance actuelle en matière de bureaux consiste à bannir les piliers afin de garantir une flexibilité de l'espace maximale. La caractéristique principale de ce bâtiment est la rampe centrale en spirale qui mène au parking et domine le hall d'entrée. La forme de la rampe se retrouve au niveau du sol revêtu de marbre et de granit. Une structure en plaques de verre fixées à des câbles en acier délimite le hall tout en établissant une certaine continuité entre l'intérieur et l'extérieur.

From left to right, from above to below:
Façade with ultra-transparent glass,
view into lobby, interior lobby.
Right: Spiral parking ramp.

Von links nach rechts, von oben nach unten:
Fassade mit ultratransparentem Glas,
Blick in die Eingangshalle, Innenansicht Eingangshalle.
Rechts: Spiralförmige Parkhausrampe.

De gauche à droite, de haut en bas:
Façade vitrée ultra transparente,
vue sur le hall d'entrée, hall d'accueil.
Droite: Rampe circulaire du parking.

# ZEAL PICTURES EUROPE,
## BERLIN, GERMANY

# GRAFT

www.graftlab.com

**Client:** ZEAL Pictures Europe, **Completion:** 2003, **Gross floor area:** 750 m², **Photos:** Torsten Seidel, Fotographie.

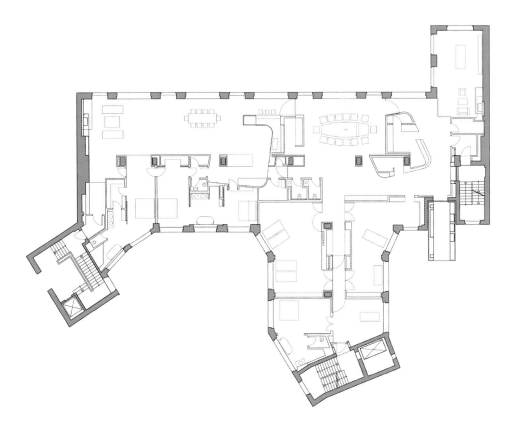

The "gate" into the loft consists of an old freight elevator that was to be demolished. GRAFT turned it into a vertical multi-media vestibule, creating an individual entry for each loft by storyboarding the experience of each client. The priority for the design was to maintain the enormous potential of the 750-m² floor plans. The living and office area thus forms one continuous space, sequenced only by two freestanding volumes. These volumes are "space shifters" that can redefine the space by moving walls and doors, which allow the creation of functional sub-entities in the ambivalent spatial design.

Das „Tor" zum Loft bildet ein Lastenaufzug, der abgerissen werden sollte. GRAFT transformierten ihn zu einem vertikalen, mobilen Empfangszimmer, das multimedial bespielt werden kann. Wesentlich für den Entwurf war, das riesige Potenzial des 750-m²-Lofts zu erhalten. So bilden der Wohn- und Bürobereich eine zusammenhängende, lediglich von zwei eingestellten Baukörpern geteilte Fläche. Diese sogenannten „space shifter" können den Raum mit Hilfe von fahrenden Wänden und Türen neu definieren und in dem ambivalenten räumlichen Entwurf funktionale Untereinheiten schaffen.

L'accès au bâtiment se fait par un ancien monte-charge que les architectes ont transformé en un vestibule sur plusieurs niveaux où des équipements multimédia présentent l'expérience de chacune des entreprises installées dans les lofts. Lors des travaux d'aménagement, la priorité consistait à conserver intactes les unités de 750 mètres carrés préexistantes. C'est pourquoi chacun de ces espaces gigantesques incluant des bureaux et des espaces de séjour n'est structuré que par deux volumes déplaçables qui constituent des sous-entités fonctionnelles modulables selon les besoins.

Loft. Dachgeschoss. Mansarde.

From left to right, from above to below:
Elevators, hallway, lobby.
Right: Interior.

Von links nach rechts, von oben nach unten:
Aufzüge, Flur, Eingangsbereich.
Rechts: Innenansicht.

De gauche à droite, de haut en bas:
Ascenseurs, couloir, hall d'entrée.
Droite: Vue de l'intérieur.

# FEDERAL BOARD OF PHYSICIANS,
## BERLIN, GERMANY

www.heinlewischerpartner.de
Client: Bavaria/IBAG Immobilien und Beteiligungen AG, Completion: 2004, Gross floor area: 13,721 m²,
Photos: Bernadette Grimmenstein.

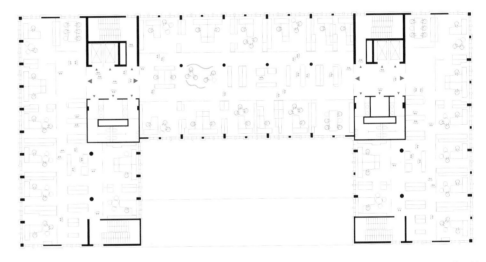

Left: Façade of natural stone. Links: Natursteinfassade. Gauche: Façade de pierre naturelle. | Right: Fourth floor plan. Rechts: Grundriss vierte Etage. Droite: plan du 4e étage.

The construction of a new representation for the Federal Board of Physicians was prompted by the development of the former site of the Royal Porcelain Factory (KPM) at the Herbert Levine square. Echoing the square's open space, the free-standing house generates a unique location profile for the new city district. The complex is designed for mixed-office use and houses 210 workplaces. Ensuring that ample sunlight reaches all offices has achieved significant energy savings. The subdivision of the modular façade's formal development is achieved with bands of natural stone.

Die neue Repräsentanz der Bundesärztekammer entstand im Rahmen der Projektentwicklung auf dem ehemaligen Gelände der Königlichen Porzellan-Manufaktur (KPM) am Herbert-Lewin-Platz. Das freistehende Haus korrespondiert mit dem Freiraum des Platzes und erzeugt ein einzigartiges Ortsprofil für den neuen Stadtteil. Der Verwaltungskomplex ist für eine Kombi-Büronutzung ausgelegt und schafft 210 Arbeitsplätze. Da in alle Büros reichlich Sonnenlicht gelangt, lassen sich signifikante Energieeinsparungen erzielen. Die formale Ausgestaltung durch eine modulare Fassadenaufteilung übernehmen Natursteinbänder.

L'Ordre des médecins allemands s'est installé sur un terrain auparavant occupé par la Manufacture royale de porcelaine (KPM). L'immeuble se dresse sur un espace dont l'aspect ouvert caractérise l'ensemble de ce quartier récemment réaménagé. Il abrite des bureaux où travaillent deux cent dix employés. L'optimisation de l'éclairage naturel permet de réaliser de substantielles économies d'énergie. Des bandes en revêtement de pierre naturelle structurent la façade modulaire du bâtiment.

From left to right, from above to below:
Spiral stairs, working spaces, entrance hall.
Right: Conference room.

Von links nach rechts, von oben nach unten:
Spiralförmige Treppe, Arbeitsplätze, Eingangshalle.
Rechts: Konferenzraum.

De gauche à droite, de haut en bas:
Escalier en colimaçon, espace de travail, hall d'entrée.
Droite: Salle de conférence.

# FINNFOREST MODULAR OFFICE,
## ESPOO, FINLAND

# HELIN & CO ARCHITECTS – PEKKA HELIN, PETER VERHE AND OTHERS

www.helinco.fi

**Client:** FMO Tapiola Real Estate Company, **Completion:** 2005, **Gross floor area:** 13,048 m², **Photos:** Voitto Niemela, Helsinki.

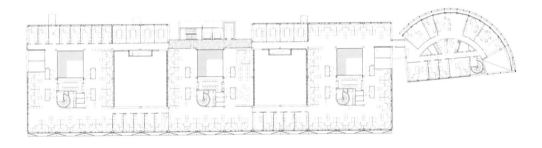

Left: East façade. Links: Ostfassade. Gauche: Façade est. | Right: Fourth floor plan. Rechts: Grundriss vierte Etage. Droite: Plan du 4e étage.

This building is the tallest timber office structure in Europe. The prefabricated, modular frame, wall and cladding units are ideal for constructing timber office buildings in individual forms. The system is based on a series of simple rectangular modules, to which curved special modules may be added. The main section of the building consists of rectangular modules, reminiscent of a stack of swan timber. The south-facing façade employs a conical module that is reminiscent of typical forms in woodworking. The workspaces are interspersed within the different modules in such a manner that all units enjoy different views.

Bei diesem Gebäude handelt es sich um das höchste Bürogebäude Europas aus Holz. Der Modulrahmen und die ebenfalls vorgefertigten Wand- und Verkleidungselemente eignen sich ideal für den Bau individuell gestalteter Bürohäuser. Das System basiert auf einer Reihe einfacher rechteckiger Module, an die sich gebogene Spezialmodule anfügen lassen. Der Haupttrakt des Gebäudes aus rechteckigen Modulen ähnelt gestapeltem Schnittholz. An der Südfassade erinnert ein kegelförmiges Modul an typische Formen der Holzbearbeitung. In den verschiedenen Modulen sind die Arbeitsplätze so verteilt, dass jede Einheit einen anderen Ausblick genießt.

Il s'agit là du plus grand immeuble en bois d'Europe. Des modules préfabriqués de forme rectangulaire ont été associés à des modules incurvés pour la structure porteuse, les façades et les murs intérieurs, avec pour résultat un immeuble de bureaux à l'aspect résolument volontaire. Le corps principal du bâtiment se compose de bandeaux qui rappellent des poutres empilées. Il se complète au sud par un volume conique qui évoque également le travail du bois. Les bureaux sont répartis de manière à offrir différentes perspectives sur la campagne environnante.

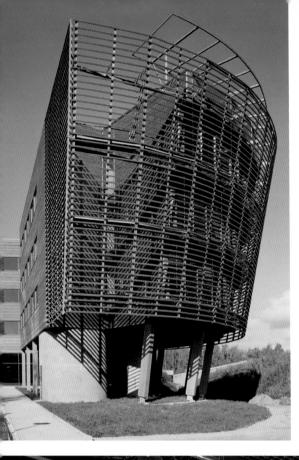

From left to right, from above to below:
South façade, detail balcony, atrium,
exterior view of atrium.
Right: South façade.

Von links nach rechts, von oben nach unten:
Südfassade, Balkondetail, Atrium,
Außenansicht Atrium.
Rechts: Südfassade.

De gauche à droite, de haut en bas:
Façade sud, balcon, atrium,
vue extérieure sur l'atrium.
Droite: Façade sud.

# CHILEXPRESS S.A.,
## SANTIAGO, CHILE

# GUILLERMO HEVIA ARQUITECTOS

www.guillermohevia.cl
Client: CHILEXPRESS S.A., Completion: 2006, Gross floor area: 7,200 m², Photos: Courtesy of Guillermo Hevia H. / Fransisco Carrión G.

Left: Glazed façade. Links: Verglaste Fassade. Gauche: Façade en verre. | Right: Typical floor plan. Rechts: Regelgeschossplan. Droite: Plan typique.

The CHILEXPRESS S.A. project incorporates an office building and a sorting and distribution center. The two buildings are connected via a "meeting square", which is accessible by all employees and culminates in a glass connection hall. The premises contain streets and interior courtyards for remote work areas. The three-floor building is distinguished by an attached glass and steel curtain façade. On the western façade, the glass parts were replaced by perforated metal sheets as sun shields coupled with transparency.

Das Projekt CHILEXPRESS S.A. umfasst ein Bürogebäude und ein Sortier- und Verteilungszentrum. Zwischen beiden Bauten vermittelt ein „Platz der Begegnung", der allen Mitarbeitern als Zugang dient und mit einer gläsernen Verbindungshalle abschließt. Die Anlage verfügt über Straßen und Innenhöfe für abgelegene Arbeitsbereiche (Erschließung und Sicherheit). Den horizontalen dreigeschossigen Baukörper prägt eine abgesetzte Vorhangfassade aus Glas und Stahl. An der Westfassade wurden die Glasteile durch perforierte Metalltafeln ersetzt, um die Sonneneinstrahlung zu mildern, ohne auf Transparenz zu verzichten.

Le projet « Chilexpress » portait sur la construction d'un immeuble de bureaux et de divers locaux techniques groupés autour de la « Place de la rencontre » où se trouve un hall d'accès vitré. Le complexe inclut également diverses cours et voies de circulation. L'immeuble de bureaux de trois étages présente une façade suspendue en panneaux de verre. Sur le côté ouest, des plaques d'acier perforées remplacent les panneaux de verre et protègent du rayonnement solaire tout en permettant un éclairage naturel de l'intérieur.

From left to right, from above to below:
Façade of glass and steel,
detail window shades, metallic panels.
Right: Exterior view.

Von links nach rechts, von oben nach unten:
Fassade aus Glas und Stahl,
Sonnenschutzdetail, metallene Paneele.
Rechts: Außenansicht.

De gauche à droite, de haut en bas:
Façade vitrée avec ossature métallique,
verre protecteur de la façade, panneaux métalliques.
Droite: Vue de l'extérieur.

# JENSEN ARCHITECTS / JENSEN & MACY ARCHITECTS

www.jensen-architects.com
**Client:** David Turner, **Completion:** 2005, **Gross floor area:** 449 m², **Photos:** Sharon Risedorph Photography.

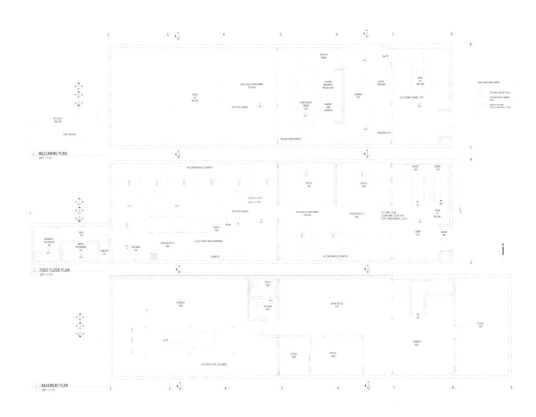

Left: Conference room. Links: Tagungsraum. Gauche: Salle de conférence. | Right: 12th floor plan. Rechts: Grundriss 12. Etage. Droite: Plan du 12e étage.

This office for a graphic design firm occupies a two-story warehouse building in the historic Jackson Square district of San Francisco. The warehouse's existing concrete shell and wood-framed roof were stripped clean, left exposed, and painted a uniform off-white. Bright, translucent red punctuates this luminous space in a series of dramatic, glass-clad rooms and structural details. The project's focal point is a heroically cantilevered glass meeting table that floats over a glass floor allowing light into the basement below. Finally, the existing brick front façade was painted black and white.

Dieses Büro einer Firma für Grafikdesign belegt ein zweigeschossiges Lagerhaus in San Franciscos Altstadtviertel Jackson Square. Die Betonschalenkonstruktion und das Fachwerkdach des Gebäudes wurden entkernt, exponiert belassen und einheitlich in einem gebrochenen Weiß gestrichen. Eine Reihe spannungsvoller, mit Glas verkleideter Räume und konstruktiver Details werden von einem hellen, transluzenten Rot akzentuiert. Blickpunkt des Projekts ist ein grandios auskragender gläserner Besprechungstisch. Er schwebt über einem Glasfußboden, durch den Licht in das Kellergeschoss darunter gelangt. Zum Schluss wurde die bestehende Backsteinfassade schwarz und weiß gestrichen.

Une société de graphisme s'est installée dans un ancien entrepôt de deux étages situé à Jackson Square, un vieux quartier de San Francisco. Les murs en béton et la charpente en bois d'origine ont été nettoyés, laissés apparents et peints en blanc cassé. Seul le rouge qu'on retrouve sur certains éléments de décor et sur les cloisons en plexiglas transparent vient ponctuer cette décoration uniformément blanche. Le point d'orgue de l'aménagement intérieur est la grande table en verre posée en équilibre au-dessus d'une plaque de verre de mêmes dimensions qui permet à la lumière naturelle de pénétrer jusqu'au sous-sol. La façade en briques est peinte en noir et blanc.

From left to right, from above to below:
Staircase, glass meeting table,
interior detail, interior view.
Right: Hallway.

Von links nach rechts, von oben nach unten:
Treppenhaus, gläserner Besprechungstisch,
Innenbereichdetail, Innenansicht.
Rechts: Flur.

De gauche à droite, de haut en bas:
Escalier, grande table verre,
détail de l'intérieur, vue de l'intérieur.
Droite: Couloir.

# KIRSHENBAUM BOND & PARTNERS WEST,
## SAN FRANCISCO, CA, USA

# JENSEN ARCHITECTS / JENSEN & MACY ARCHITECTS

www.jensen-architects.com
**Client:** Chuck Maggio CFO, **Completion:** 2001, **Gross floor area:** 2,093 m², **Photos:** Courtesy of Jensen Architects.

Left: Conference room. Links: Konferenzraum. Gauche: Salle de conférence. | Right: Floor plans. Rechts: Grundrisse. Droite: Plans.

A unique three-wing conference building serves as the focal point of this office for advertising agency Kirshenbaum Bond & Partners West. The structure houses four meeting rooms, each with an unique configuration and material quality. At the center of the office is a green carpet-clad phone booth structure for conference calls. Other special features include an indoor garden, a sixteen foot dining counter, and a stadium stair that, in addition to providing access to the mezzanine, becomes a place for company-wide meetings and informal gatherings.

Ein ungewöhnliches dreiflügeliges Konferenzgebäude dient der Werbeagentur Kirshenbaum Bond & Partners West als Zentrum. Es beherbergt vier Konferenzräume mit jeweils spezifischer Gestaltung und Materialqualität. Die Mitte des Büros nimmt eine mit grünem Teppichboden ausgekleidete Telefonzellen-Konstruktion für Konferenzschaltungen ein. Weitere besondere Merkmale sind ein Innengarten, eine 4,90 Meter lange Esstheke und eine Stadiontreppe, die nicht nur das Zwischengeschoss erschließt, sondern auch unternehmensweite Begegnungen und zwanglose Treffen ermöglicht.

L'agence de publicité Kirshenbaum Bond & Partner West est installée dans ce bâtiment en trois volumes. On y trouve quatre salles de réunion, chacune étant caractérisée par des matériaux et une configuration qui lui sont propres. Au centre de l'agence se trouve un espace moquetté en vert réservé aux téléconférences. Citons encore parmi les aménagements un jardin intérieur, une table pour banquets de cinq mètres de long et des gradins qui donnent accès à la mezzanine et servent lors des réunions informelles ou des assemblées générales du personnel.

From left to right, from above to below:
Green carpet-clad phone booth structure, meeting pool,
conference room, detail wall cladding.
Right: Indoor garden.

Von links nach rechts, von oben nach unten:
Verkleidung Telefonkabinen: Kunstrasen, Aufenthaltsraum,
Konferenzraum, Detail Wandverkleidung.
Rechts: Innengarten.

De gauche à droite, de haut en bas:
Cabines de téléphones avec structures peintes en vert,
salle d'attente, salle de conférence, détail du mur.
Droite: Jardin intérieur.

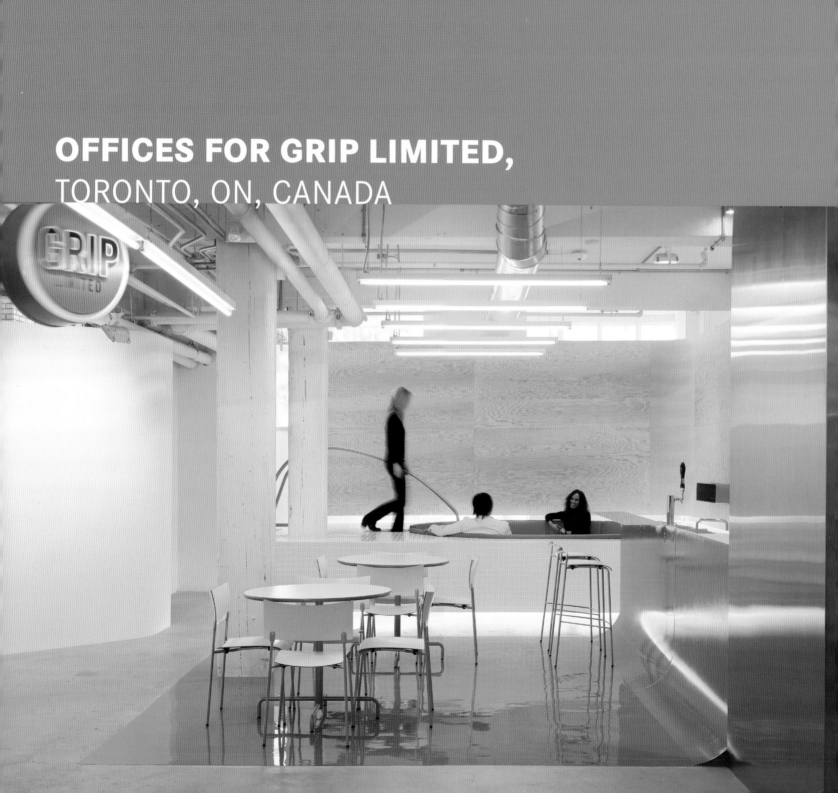

# OFFICES FOR GRIP LIMITED,
## TORONTO, ON, CANADA

# JOHNSON CHOU

www.johnsonchou.com
**Client:** Grip Limited, **Completion:** 2006, **Gross floor area:** 2,000 m², **Photos:** Tom Arban Photography.

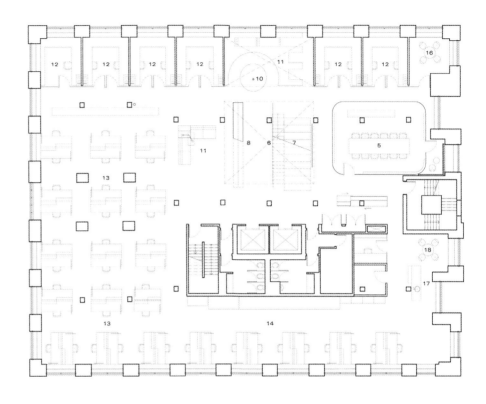

Left: "Hot Tub" meeting area. Links: „Hot Tub" Aufenthaltsraum. Gauche: Salle d'accueil „Hot Tub". | Right: Fifth floor plan. Rechts: Grundriss Fünfte Etage. Droite: Plan du 5e étage.

The formal and informal meeting spaces throughout the agency offer various spatial experiences. The double-height atrium visually and functionally links the two main floors. In addition to a stairway related to the bleachers, vertical movement is also provided by a slide and a fire-pole connecting the creative offices. Made of folded hot-rolled steel and stained walnut veneer, the bleachers are used for full office meetings, film presentations and as an alternative workplace, while the meeting area resembles a large hot tub. Clad in stainless steel, the interior is finished with white synthetic grass.

Die formellen und informellen Besprechungsbereiche der Agentur bieten verschiedene räumliche Erfahrungen. Das Atrium mit doppelter Raumhöhe vermittelt optisch und funktionell zwischen den beiden Hauptgeschossen. Außer einer Treppe in Gestalt einer Tribüne verbinden eine Rutsche und eine Feuerwehrstange die Büros der Kreativen. Die Tribüne aus gebogenem Walzstahl und gebeiztem Nussbaumfurnier wird für Mitarbeiterversammlungen, Filmvorführungen und als alternativer Arbeitsplatz genutzt. Die Besprechungszone erinnert an einen Whirlpool. Verkleidungen aus Edelstahl und weißer Kunstrasen runden die Ausstattung ab.

Divers lieux pour des réunions formelles ou informelles sont répartis à l'intérieur de cette agence. Une verrière sur deux niveaux interconnecte les deux étages principaux. Les déplacements verticaux entre les bureaux des créateurs se font non seulement par l'escalier et les gradins, mais aussi par un toboggan et une perche de pompier. Les gradins en acier recouvert de noyer servent lors des réunions du personnel et des projections de films. La salle de réunion proprement dite ressemble à un grand tuyau. Les aménagements intérieurs sont en acier inox et en verre synthétique blanc.

Interior slide and pole. Innenansicht Rutsche und Stange. Vue sur le toboggan et la rampe verticale.

From left to right, from above to below:
Entrance to conference room, staircase and slide.
Right: View towards reception / waiting pod.

Von links nach rechts, von oben nach unten:
Eingang zum Konferenzraum, Treppe und Rutsche.
Rechts: Blick auf die Rezeption / Wartebereich.

De gauche à droite, de haut en bas:
Entrée de la salle de conférence, escalier et toboggan.
Droite: Vue sur la réception / salle d'attente.

# RED BULL HEADQUARTERS,
## LONDON, UNITED KINGDOM

# JUMP STUDIOS

www.jump-studios.com
**Client:** Red Bull UK Ltd., **Completion:** 2006, **Gross floor area:** 1,860 m², **Photos:** Garth Gardner.

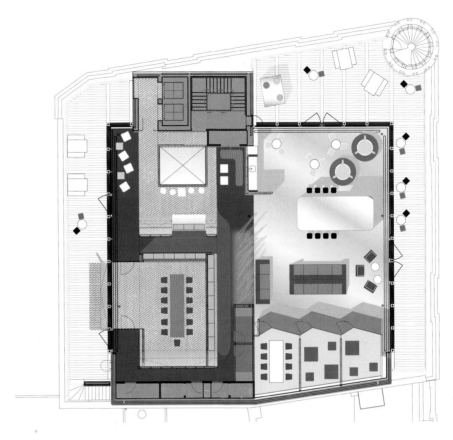

Left: Bar in kitchen and lounge area. Links: Bar im Küchen- und Loungebereich. Gauche: Bar dans l'espace de la cuisine et de la mansarde. | Right: Floor plan. Rechts: Grundriss. Droite: Plan.

Encouraging interaction between employees while communicating the company's brand values were the dual aims of the design of Red Bull's new 1,860 m² headquarters. The brief was to amalgamate two separate offices into one central headquarters building. Employees and visitors arrive by lift into this top-floor public reception and social zone, before descending through the building. This sense of descent is enhanced by voids punched through the building fabric. These contain dramatic means of circulation via a floating staircase and even a slide, aimed at encouraging free movement through the space.

Die Kommunikation zwischen den Mitarbeitern zu fördern und die Markenwerte des Unternehmens zu vermitteln, lauteten die Ziele des Entwurfs für eine neue 1.860 m² große Hauptverwaltung von Red Bull. Zwei getrennte Bürotrakte sollten zu einem zentralen Verwaltungsgebäude vereint werden. Beschäftigte und Besucher erreichen die Empfangs- und Begegnungszone im Dachgeschoss. Anschließend begeben sie sich hinab durch das Gebäude. Im Baukörper ausgesparte Hohlräume verstärken den Eindruck eines Abstiegs. Sie enthalten ein spektakuläres Erschließungssystem mit einer schwebenden Treppe und sogar einer Rutsche zur ungehinderten Fortbewegung im Raum.

Le nouveau siège social de Red Bull, qui couvre 1860 mètres carrés, a été aménagé en fonction de deux objectifs principaux : favoriser l'interaction entre les employés et communiquer les valeurs clés de l'entreprise. Les travaux ont porté sur la réunion de deux bâtiments distincts afin de former une seule unité spatiale. L'accès à la zone d'accueil se fait par ascenseur, et l'on doit redescendre pour rejoindre les différents bureaux. Plusieurs puis répartis dans l'immeuble soulignent ce mouvement du haut vers le bas. On y trouve notamment un escalier flottant et un toboggan dont le but est d'encourager la liberté de mouvement à travers l'espace.

Interior level 5. Innenansicht 5. Etage. Vue du 5e étage.

From left to right, from above to below:
Floating staircase, meeting room,
lounge area, stair and slide connection.
Right: Reception.

Von links nach rechts, von oben nach unten:
Schwebende Treppe, Aufenthaltsraum,
Loungebereich, Treppe und Rutsche.
Rechts: Empfang.

De gauche à droite, de haut en bas:
Escalier flottant, salle de réunion,
mansarde, espace entre l'escalier et le toboggan.
Droite: Réception.

# ENGINE,
## LONDON, UNITED KINGDOM

# JUMP STUDIOS

www.jump-studios.com

**Client:** Engine, **Completion:** 2008, **Gross floor area:** 5,485 m², **Photos:** Garth Gardner.

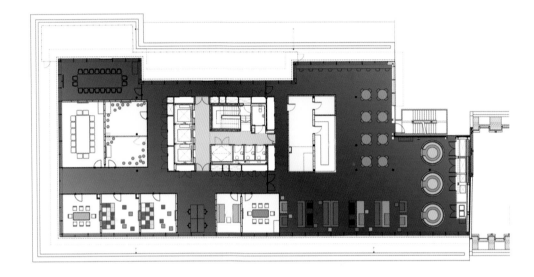

Left: Entrance view. Links: Eingangsbereich. Gauche: Vue sur l'entrée. | Right: Floor plan. Rechts: Grundriss. Droite: Plan d'ensemble.

The challenge was to create an environment that would appeal to many tastes while respecting individual brand identities. A dramatic element is the floating auditorium at entrance level, designed for presentations. The 'talking points' in the building include the seating pods on the fifth floor with Corian shells and Barrisol light ceilings where employees can interact in a series of conference and meeting rooms ranging in design, size and style. Imaginative solutions include 'mini auditorium' seating systems and a room clad entirely in cork (with matching cork stools) for quick temporary interactions.

Zu gestalten war ein Umfeld, das jedem Geschmack zusagen und gleichzeitig den spezifischen Marken-identitäten gerecht würde. Auf der Eingangsebene liefert das für Präsentationen bestimmte schwe-bende Auditorium ein dramatisches Element. Zu den kommunikativen Knotenpunkten im Gebäude zählen die Sitzinseln im fünften Geschoss mit Einfas-sungen aus Corian und Barrisol-Lichtdecken. Hier können die Mitarbeiter in mehreren Konferenz- und Besprechungszimmern unterschiedlicher Gestaltung, Größe und Stilrichtung miteinander kommunizieren. Fantasievoll umgesetzt wurden die Sitzsysteme „Mini-Auditorium" sowie ein vollständig mit Kork ausgekleideter Raum für spontane Begegnungen.

La difficulté consistait ici à créer un environnement qui réponde à des goûts différents tout en respec-tant l'identité de plusieurs entreprises. L'élément dominant est l'auditorium de l'entrée, utilisé pour les présentations. Parmi les points de rencontre répartis à l'intérieur du bâtiment, citons notamment les espaces du cinquième étage : bien que leur taille et leur décoration soient toujours différentes, tous ces espaces sont dotés de sièges en Corian® et de plafonds lumineux Barrisol®. Parmi les solutions no-vatrices, citons pour terminer le « mini-auditorium » et la salle aux murs entièrement recouverts de liège, où se trouvent des tabourets également en liège.

Entrance hall. Eingangshalle. Hall d'entrée.

From left to right, from above to below:
Informal meeting space, cafeteria,
light installation in waiting zone, meeting room.
Right: Cafeteria.

Von links nach rechts, von oben nach unten:
Formloser Treffpunkt, Cafeteria,
Lichtinstallation im Wartebereich, Aufenthaltsraum.
Rechts: Cafeteria.

De gauche à droite, de haut en bas:
Point de rencontre, cafétéria, installations lumineuses
dans la salle d'attente, salle de réunion.
Droite: Cafétéria.

# COMPANY HEADQUARTERS FOR CLASSICON GMBH,
## MUNICH, GERMANY

# JOACHIM JÜRKE ARCHITECTS

www.jarch.de

**Client:** ClassiCon GmbH, **Completion:** 2001, **Gross floor area:** 2000 m², **Photos:** Hubertus Hamm, Munich.

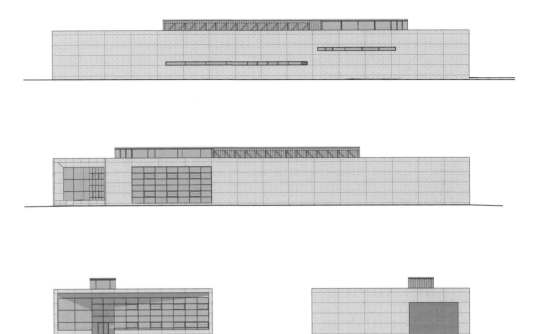

Left: Glass and concrete façade. Links: Fassade aus Glas und Beton. Gauche: Façade de béton et de verre. | Right: Elevations. Rechts: Ansichten. Droite: Élévations.

The orientation of the offices and the showroom towards the South and the delivery department towards the North can be seen as a logical consequence of the different needs and requirements of these sections. The generous opening towards the South, contrasting with the otherwise monolithic structure, emphasizes this concept even more. A main axis, taking visitors from South to North from the entry ramp via the staircase to the warehouse and from there to the open air loading yard, presents a view across the entire building when the sliding gate is open.

Die Ausrichtung der Büros sowie des Showrooms nach Süden beziehungsweise der Anlieferung nach Norden kann als logische Folgerung auf die unterschiedlichen Bedürfnisse und Anforderungen dieser Bereiche verstanden werden. Die großzügige Öffnung nach Süden unterstreicht diese Haltung im Gegensatz zu dem ansonsten monolithisch gehaltenen Baukörper nochmals. Eine Hauptachse, die den Betrachter von Süden nach Norden über die Eingangsrampe durch das Treppenhaus in die Lagerhalle und von dort in den nicht überdachten Ladehof führt, ermöglicht bei geöffnetem Schiebetor einen Durchblick durch das gesamte Gebäude.

Les différents espaces ont ici une orientation qui correspond à leur fonction : bureaux et salles d'exposition au sud, réception des marchandises au nord. Le bâtiment perd son aspect monolithique sur la façade sud, qui s'ouvre largement sur l'extérieur. Une porte coulissante offre une vue en perspective de l'intérieur selon cet axe sud-nord, qui correspond également à la voie de circulation interne qui va de la rampe d'accès à la cour de chargement en passant par l'escalier et le magasin.

From left to right, from above to below:
Interior view, workspace, staircase.
Right: South façade.

Von links nach rechts, von oben nach unten:
Innenansicht, Arbeitsraum, Treppe.
Rechts: Südfassade.

De gauche à droite, de haut en bas:
Vue de l'intérieur, salle de travail, escalier.
Droite: Façade sud.

# DESIGN OFFICE KMS TEAM,
## MUNICH, GERMANY

# JOACHIM JÜRKE ARCHITECTS

www.jarch.de
**Client:** KMS, **Completion:** 2007, **Gross floor area:** 2,900 m², **Photos:** Holger Albricht, Joachim Jürke.

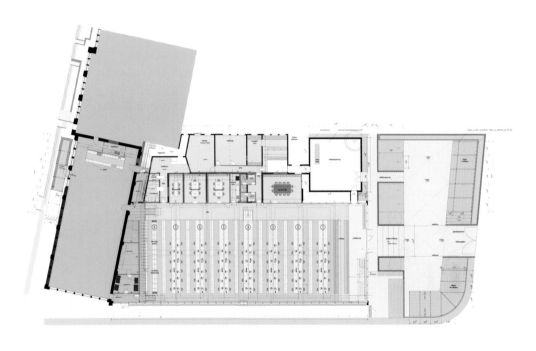

Left: Entrance. Links: Eingang. Gauche: Entrée. | Right: Floor plan. Rechts: Grundriss. Droite: Plan d'ensemble.

The plan called for reconstituting and highlighting the initial character of the industrial hall. The work processes and the room climate were also to be enhanced. This effect was achieved by the addition of an air-conditioned work platform. The formal strength of the rows was diluted within the groups, resulting in a feeling of belonging to the applicable common project.

Der ursprüngliche Charakter der Industriehalle sollte wiederhergestellt und herausgearbeitet werden. Dazu sollten die Arbeitsabläufe ebenso wie das Raumklima optimiert werden, welches durch das Einschieben einer klimatisierten Arbeitsplattform erreicht wurde. Die formale Strenge der Zeilen löst sich innerhalb der Gruppen auf und es entsteht das Gefühl der Zusammengehörigkeit zu dem jeweiligen gemeinschaftlichen Projekt.

Des travaux de réhabilitation ont rendu à ce bâtiment industriel son aspect d'origine. Ils visaient également à optimiser les processus productifs et les conditions climatiques à l'intérieur de la halle grâce à la construction d'une plate-forme climatisée. La rigidité formelle des rangées y est pondérée par des regroupements qui favorisent la sensation de travail en commun sur les divers projets.

K4

From left to right, from above to below:
Aerial view hall, conference room,
view point "blackbox".
Right: "Pit lane".

Von links nach rechts, von oben nach unten:
Überblick der Halle, Besprechungsraum,
Standpunkt „Blackbox".
Rechts: „Boxengasse".

De gauche à droite, de haut en bas:
Vue aérienne du hall, salle de conférence,
point de vue „blackbox".
Droite: Bureaux vitrés.

# F-ZEIN OFFICES,

## ATHENS, GREECE

# KLAB ARCHITECTS

www.klmf.gr

**Client:** F-Zein Company, **Completion:** 2005, **Gross floor area:** 700 m², **Photos:** B. Louzidis.

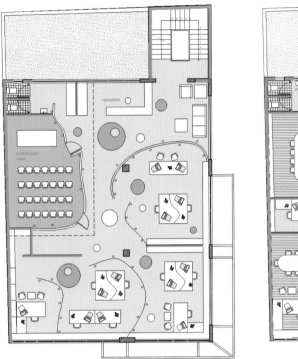 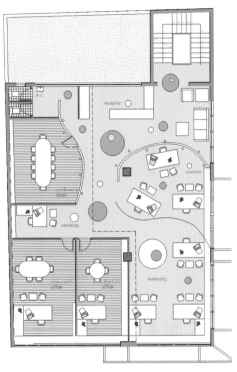

Left: Lobby. Links: Empfang. Gauche: Accueil. | Right: Ground floor and first floor plan. Rechts: Grundriss Erdgeschoss und erste Etage. Droite: Plan du rez-de-chaussée et du 1er étage.

The architectural design of the "fzin" offices included the exterior renovation and interior refurbishment of an old industrial building, finally creating an interesting working environment with flexible, almost liquid spaces, which can continually be transformed and reordered. KLAB architects emphasized a fresh and experimental design with the use of special and unusual materials.

Zur architektonischen Gestaltung der „fzin"-Büros gehörte neben dem Umbau auch die Renovierung des Interieurs eines alten Fabrikgebäudes. Entstanden ist eine interessante Arbeitsumgebung mit flexiblen, nahezu fließenden Räumen, die sich immer wieder umgestalten und neu ordnen lassen. KLAB Architects verliehen mit besonderen und ausgefallenen Materialien einem frischen und experimentellen Entwurf Nachdruck.

La tâche des architectes consistait à rénover l'intérieur et l'extérieur d'un ancien bâtiment industriel, et à créer des bureaux dotés d'une atmosphère de travail agréable. Les nouveaux espaces se définissent par leur caractère flexible et presque fluide qui permet une réorganisation spatiale sans problèmes. La décoration fraîche et expérimentale qui a été retenue privilégie l'usage de matériaux inhabituels.

From left to right, from above to below:
Flexible workspaces, staircase, interior of corrugated
polyester rolls and galvanized steel disks on ceiling.
Right: Conference room.

Von links nach rechts, von oben nach unten:
Flexible Arbeitsräume, Treppe, Innenansicht aus geriffelten
Polyesterrollen und Scheiben aus verzinktem Stahl.
Rechts: Tagungsraum.

De gauche à droite, de haut en bas:
Espaces de travail flexibles, escalier, intérieur fait de rouleaux de
polyester plissé et de disques d'acier galvanisé au plafond.
Droite: Salle de conférence.

# KANGAROOS HEADQUARTERS,
## PIRMASENS, GERMANY

# LANDAU AND KINDELBACHER ARCHITECTS – INTERIOR DESIGNER

www.landaukindelbacher.de

**Client:** Bernd Hummel GmbH, **Completion:** 2005, **Gross floor area:** 2,150 m², **Photos:** Florian Holzherr, Munich.

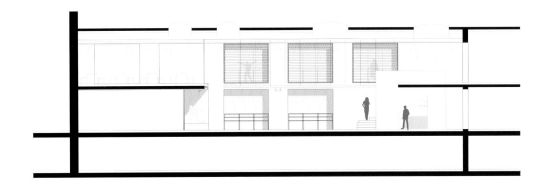

Left: Conference room. Links: Tagungsraum. Gauche: Salle de conférence. | Right: Longitudinal section. Rechts: Längsschnitt. Droite: Coupe longitudinale.

The preservation of the original building fabric and the inclusion of functional fittings for modern offices dominate the concept; fair-faced masonry featuring the sandstone typical of the region and a light-gray coating on the floors, walls and ceilings runs through the building like a red thread. Wall-to-ceiling astragal windows produce a special atmosphere for the creative minds. An open area and the "Big Show" are used as cafeteria, exhibition area, meeting room and product presentation. The combination of modern entrepreneurial culture and a successful reminiscence of an old industrial monument breathe new life into the former bel etage.

Die Erhaltung der historischen Bausubstanz und funktionale Einbauten für moderne Büronutzung bestimmen das Konzept. Sichtmauerwerk aus dem typischen regionalen Sandstein, dazu lichtgraue Beschichtung an Böden, Wänden und Decken ziehen sich wie ein roter Faden durch das Gebäude. Raumhohe Sprossenfenster schaffen für die kreativen Köpfe eine besondere Atmosphäre. Eine offene Kommunikationszone und die „Big Show" dienen als Cafeteria, Ausstellungsfläche, Besprechungsraum und zur Produktpräsentation. Die Kombination aus moderner Unternehmenskultur und die gelungene Reminiszenz an ein altes Industriedenkmal erwecken die ehemalige Beletage zu neuem Leben.

Le projet consistait ici principalement à moderniser le bâtiment tout en conservant la structure d'origine. Les caractéristiques principales de la réalisation sont l'usage du grès – un matériau typique de la région – et la teinte gris clair qu'on retrouve sur les murs, le sol et le plafond. Des fenêtres à astragale créent une atmosphère particulière dans les bureaux des créatifs. L'espace ouvert baptisé « Big Show », qui abrite la cafétéria, sert également pour les réunions, les expositions et les présentations de produits. Ces aménagements inspirés par un esprit d'entreprise moderne ont donné une nouvelle vie à un ancien bâtiment industriel.

From left to right, from above to below:
Office area, reception area, meeting areas.
Right: View of conference room with sky canopy.

Von links nach rechts, von oben nach unten:
Büro, Empfang, Aufenthaltsraum.
Rechts: Blick auf den Tagungsraum mit Himmelverkleidung.

De gauche à droite, de haut en bas:
Bureaux, réception, salle d'accueil.
Droite: Vue sur la salle de conférence avec faux plafond en ciel.

# PRIVATE EQUITY FIRM,
## MUNICH, GERMANY

LANDAU AND KINDELBACHER
ARCHITECTS – INTERIOR DESIGNER

www.landaukindelbacher.de
**Completion:** 2007, **Gross floor area:** 800 m², **Photos:** Christian Hacker, Munich.

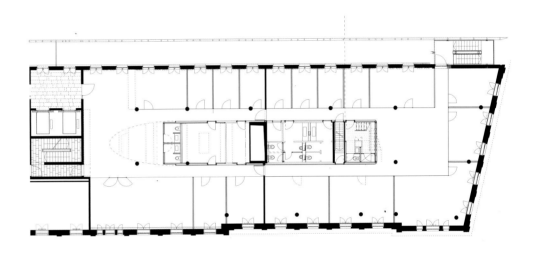

Left: Conference room. Links: Tagungsraum. Gauche: Salle de conférence. | Right: Floor plan. Rechts: Grundriss. Droite: Plan.

The office reconstruction for a luxury financial services provider completes the interior work in the Bürklein building / Maximilianhof. The implementation of the classical River boat theme with choice materials and a clear-cut design set new standards. Boarded floors with stainless steel inlays, glossily painted walls and doors, coupled with high-quality exotic woods reflect the customer's desire for a unique room experience. The visible steel girders of the roof construction add dynamism to the room, while the balcony along the full length of the building offers a great view of the city.

Der Umbau für einen Finanzdienstleister im oberen Luxussegment komplettiert den Innenausbau der Büroflächen im Bürkleinbau / Maximilianhof. Die Umsetzung des klassischen River-Boat-Themas in Materialwahl und Formensprache setzt neue Maßstäbe. Dielenboden mit Edelstahleinlagen, lackierte Wände und Türen, der Einbau von hochwertigen Edelhölzern spiegeln den Wunsch des Bauherrn nach einem einzigartigen Raumerlebnis wider. Die sichtbaren Stahlträger der Dachkonstruktion verleihen dem Raum zusätzliche Dynamik.

Un prestataire de services financiers haut de gamme a chargé les architectes de moderniser ses bureaux situés dans un quartier chic de Munich en réinterprétant un grand classique : le style paquebot. Des parquets avec incrustations d'acier inox, des portes et des murs laqués, ainsi que l'usage d'essences précieuses créent ici une atmosphère exceptionnellement luxueuse. Les poutres en acier laissées apparentes confèrent d'autre part un dynamisme particulier aux aménagements intérieurs.

Lobby. Empfang. Accueil.

From left to right, from above to below:
Hallway, conference room, lobby, hallway.
Right: Lounge area.

Von links nach rechts, von oben nach unten:
Flur, Tagungsraum, Empfang, Flur.
Rechts: Loungebereich.

De gauche à droite, de haut en bas:
Couloir, salle de conférence, espace d'accueil, couloir.
Droite: Coin repos.

# KILNCRAIGS MILL REDEVELOPMENT,
## ALLOA, UNITED KINGDOM

# LDN ARCHITECTS

www.ldn.co.uk

**Client:** Clackmanshire Council, **Completion:** 2003, **Gross floor area:** 9,825 m², **Photos:** Peter Iain Campbell Photography.

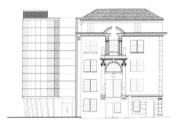

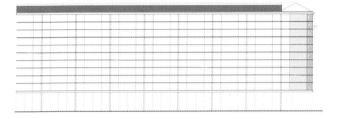

Left: View from south-east. Links: Blick aus Süd-Osten. Gauche: Façade sud-est. | Right: East and south elevation. Rechts: Ost- und Südansicht. Droite: Élévations est et sud.

This deceptively simple design converted the two remaining buildings of a former woolmill to form a new Center of Creative Industries. The unequivocally contemporary design of the atrium acts as a foil to architecture of the earlier buildings and adds a 21st century element to the historical development of the site. The dramatic new glass façade is symbolic of the renewal of the buildings and of Alloa town center itself. The redevelopment is recognized as being a catalyst for the regeneration of the surrounding area.

Dieser vermeintlich einfache Entwurf verwandelte die beiden verbliebenen Gebäude einer ehemaligen Wollspinnerei in ein Zentrum der kreativen Branchen. Das unmissverständlich moderne Atrium dient als Hintergrund für die zwei alten Bauten und ergänzt die historische Bebauung des Standorts um ein Element aus dem 21. Jahrhundert. Die aufsehenerregende neue Glasfassade symbolisiert die Wiederherstellung der Gebäude und auch des Stadtzentrums von Alloa. Die Sanierung gilt als Katalysator für die Erneuerung der Umgebung.

La conversion en un centre de design de deux bâtiments abritant autrefois une filature s'est faite en utilisant une solution simple au possible. Une façade en verre d'un style ultramoderne symbolise le renouveau du centre ville d'Alloa et projette dans le XXIe siècle les deux immeubles classés bâtiments historiques. Ce projet architectural a dynamisé la modernisation de tout le quartier.

Fully glazed façade. Vollständig verglaste Fassade. Façade entièrement vitrée.

From left to right, from above to below:
Corporate symbol, lobby,
atrium entrance, staircase.
Right: Entrance view.

Von links nach rechts, von oben nach unten:
Firmenlogo, Empfang, E
ingang Atrium, Treppe.
Rechts: Blick auf den Eingang.

De gauche à droite, de haut en bas:
Logo de l'entreprise, accueil,
entrée de l'atrium, escalier.
Droite: Vue sur l'entrée.

# LEHRER OFFICE,
## LOS ANGELES, CA, USA

# LEHRER ARCHITECTS

www.lehrerarchitects.com

**Client:** Lehrer Architects , **Completion:** 2005, **Gross floor area:** 501 m², **Photos:** Benny Chan / Fotoworks, Los Angeles (156, 158, 159, 160 a.l., 160 b., 161), Michael B. Lehrer, FAIA, Los Angeles (160 a.r.).

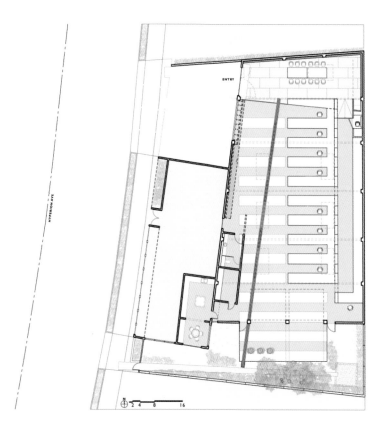

Left: Conference room. Links: Tagungsraum. Gauche: Salle de conférence. | Right: Floor plan. Rechts: Grundriss. Droite: Plan.

The project included succinct interventions to become a working space of light, air, and transparency. Although the office would specifically house architects, the architects designed a multipurpose working space that simply and clearly honors the rudiments of work: vast work surfaces, massive natural light, seamless connections to the landscape and fresh air, generous storage, and clearly individuated workstations that add up to a coherent, palpable group. The space succeeds as an open, collaborative working lab for creative design.

Bei diesem Projekt entstand durch wenige gezielte Eingriffe ein von Licht, Luft und Transparenz bestimmter Arbeitsraum. Obwohl in diesem Büro insbesondere Architekten tätig sein sollten, entwarfen Lehrer Architects einen vielseitig verwendbaren Arbeitsplatz. Er erfüllt unkompliziert und deutlich die Grundvoraussetzungen des Arbeitens: ausgedehnte Arbeitsflächen, eine Fülle natürlichen Lichts, nahtlose Verbindungen zur Landschaft und zur frischen Luft, großzügige Ablagen und eindeutig individualisierte Arbeitsstationen, die zu einer in sich geschlossenen augenfälligen Gruppe beitragen. Der Raum überzeugt als offener Bereich für kooperative Experimente im kreativen Design.

Des interventions ponctuelles ont fait de ce lieu un espace de clarté et de transparence. Bien qu'il abrite un bureau d'architectes, la bâtiment pourrait aussi bien servir à d'autres activités professionnelles. Toujours est-il qu'il intègre ce qui caractérise l'architecture intérieure moderne : vastes espaces de travail, usage intensif de l'éclairage naturel, intégration du paysage, ventilation naturelle, bonnes capacités de rangement et postes de travail personnalisés. Avec pour résultat un laboratoire qui favorise le travail en équipe et la créativité.

Interior with view toward garden. Innenansicht mit Blick in Richtung Garten. Vue intérieure avec perspective sur le jardin.

From left to right, from above to below:
View of garden, view of interior from garden, interior.
Right: Workstations.

Von links nach rechts, von oben nach unten:
Blick in den Garten, Innenansicht von der Gartenseite, Innenansicht.
Rechts: Arbeitsplätze.

De gauche à droite, de haut en bas:
Vue sur le jardin, vue de l'intérieur depuis le jardin, intérieur.
Droite: Espaces de travail.

# DAIMLERCHRYSLER SERVICES,
## BERLIN, GERMANY

# MARTINI, MEYER

www.martinimeyer.com

**Client:** DaimlerChrysler Services Mobility Management, **Completion:** 2003, **Gross floor area:** approx. 150 m², **Photos:** Courtesy of MARTINI, MEYER.

Left: Lobby. Links: Empfangsbereich. Gauche: Accueil. | Right: Perspective. Rechts: Ansicht. Droite: Perspective.

MARTINI, MEYER developed the design for the entry area of the DaimlerChrysler Services Mobility Management at the Potsdamer Platz in Berlin. Unlimited and infinite is the reception desk running through the glas wall in the entrance area. The design of the bar bases on the concept of natural movement and communicates boundlessness, both key issues of the enterprise. Through organically shaped elements the premises on the 6th and the 8th floor are referring to eachother. The project was made in cooperation with the agency Zum goldenen Hirschen Berlin.

MARTINI, MEYER entwickelten den Empfangsbereichs des neuen Büros von DaimlerChysler Services Mobility Management am Potsdamer Platz. Die natürliche Form des Tresenverlaufs kommuniziert reibungslose Abläufe im Raum. Die Formsprache greift das Konzept der Bewegung auf und veranschaulicht Grenzenlosigkeit. Die Räumlichkeiten der 6. und 8. Etage korrespondieren anhand organisch verlaufender räumlicher Elemente inhaltlich und gestalterisch. Das Projekt ist in Kooperation mit der Agentur Zum goldenen Hirschen Berlin entstanden.

MARTINI, MEYER a élaboré la conception pour le champ de saisie de la gestion de mobilité de services de DaimlerChrysler chez le Potsdamer Platz à Berlin. La forme naturelle du comptoir communique déroulements bons dans le secteur. La langue de forme reprend le concept du mouvement et illustre de immensité. Ce concept décoratif se retrouve au sixième et au huitième étage de l'immeuble, qui abrite également la société DaimlerChrysler Services Mobility Management. Le projet a été mené en collaboration avec l'agence berlinoise Zum goldenen Hirschen.

TOLL COLLECT

From left to right, from above to below:
Interior, lobby, corporate logo.
Right: Lobby.

Von links nach rechts, von oben nach unten:
Innenansicht, Empfangsbereich, Firmenlogo.
Rechts: Empfangsbereich.

De gauche à droite, de haut en bas:
Intérieur, lieu d'accueil, logo de la firme.
Droite: Accueil.

# SOLID:FLOW,
## BERLIN, GERMANY

# MARTINI, MEYER

www.martinimeyer.com
**Client:** Product Visionaires GmbH, **Completion:** 2005, **Gross floor area:** 1,100 m², **Photos:** Arwed Messmer.

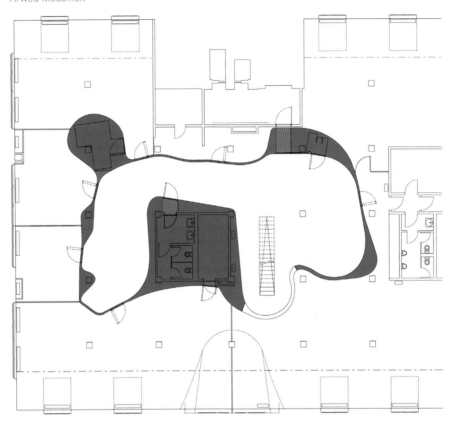

Left: Interior with light installations. Links: Innenansicht mit Lichtinstallation. Gauche: Intérieur avec installations lumineuses. | Right: Sixth floor plan. Rechts: Grundriss Sechste Etage. Droite: Plan du 6e étage.

The interplay of "solid and flow," transparency and density resulted in a very creative outcome. The organic room-in-room-concept with perforated walls provides various functions according to the needs of each area. The surface is made of walnut wood, creating an intimate atmosphere within the lively and transparent office rooms. The loops of the wooden form are further key elements of the design. Apparently playful, the design is actually functional and suited to the needs of a progressive and sophisticated communication company, which is linked to the world and works on very complex tasks.

Das Wechselspiel von „solide und fließend", Transparenz und Dichte führte zu einem sehr kreativen Ergebnis. Das organische Raum-im-Raum-Konzept mit Durchbrüchen in den Wänden bietet verschiedene Funktionen je nach Bedarf der einzelnen Bereiche. Oberflächen aus Walnussholz erzeugen eine vertraute Atmosphäre in den belebten und transparenten Büroräumen. Die geschwungene Form aus Holz bildet ein weiteres Schlüsselelement des Designs. Auch wenn die Gestaltung verspielt erscheint, ist sie in Wirklichkeit funktional und den Bedürfnissen eines progressiven und hochentwickelten Kommunikationsunternehmens angepasst, das mit der Welt in Verbindung steht und an sehr komplexen Aufgaben arbeitet.

L'interaction du solide et du liquide, de la transparence et de la densité a pour résultat un immeuble au design hautement novateur. Un concept organique « pièce dans la pièce », utilisant des cloisons perforées, permet d'adapter l'espace aux besoins du client. Le revêtement mural en noyer crée une atmosphère d'intimité dans ces bureaux à la fois vivants et transparents. Les ondulations des cloisons sont un élément clé du concept choisi. Malgré son apparence bon enfant, cette décoration intérieure est fonctionnelle et parfaitement adaptée aux exigences d'une entreprise de communication globale qui réalise des tâches extrêmement complexes.

Lobby. Empfang. Accueil.

From left to right, from above to below:
Lounge, workstation, open office.
Right: Lounge.

Von links nach rechts, von oben nach unten:
Lounge, Arbeitsplatz, offene Bürolandschaft.
Rechts: Lounge.

De gauche à droite, de haut en bas:
Mansarde, espace de travail, open spaces.
Droite: Lounge.

# ROTHOBLAAS,
## BOZEN, ITALY

# MONOVOLUME

www.monovolume.cc
**Client:** Blaas OHG, **Completion:** 2005, **Gross floor area:** 1,250 m², **Photos:** Oskar Da Riz, Bozen.

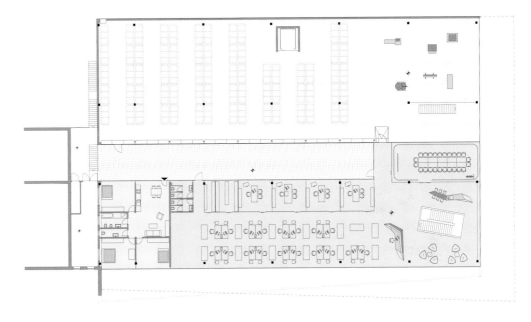

Left: Lobby. Links: Empfang. Gauche: Accueil. | Right: Floor plan. Rechts: Grundriss. Droite: Plan.

Rothoblaas is a large-scale commercial operation specializing in assembling systems and power tools for the woodworking industry. Warehouse and commissioning are situated on the ground floor whereas administration, a meeting room and a showroom can be found on the upper floor. The aim of the project was to create a compact building with a high recognition value, a building that serves as an embodiment of the enterprise's contemporary corporate identity. This has lead to a functional, compact structural shell, provided with a glass envelope. The main building material employed is wood to showcase the company's own products.

Rothoblaas ist ein großes, auf Elektrowerkzeuge und Montagesysteme für die Holzindustrie spezialisiertes Handelsunternehmen. Lager und Versand befinden sich im Erdgeschoss, die Verwaltung sowie ein Konferenzzimmer und ein Ausstellungsraum im Obergeschoss. Ziel des Projekts war, ein kompaktes Gebäude mit hohem Wiedererkennungswert zu schaffen. Das Gebäude sollte die zeitgemäße und repräsentative CI des Unternehmens darstellen, was zu einer funktionalen, kompakten Struktur und gläsernen Hülle führte. Hauptmaterial ist jedoch das auf das Tätigkeitsfeld verweisende Holz.

Rothoblaas est un revendeur d'outils électriques et de systèmes de montage pour l'industrie du bois. Le magasin et la centrale d'expédition se trouvent au rez-de-chaussée, les bureaux — complétés par une salle de conférence et un espace d'exposition — occupant le premier étage. La tâche des architectes consistait à réaliser un bâtiment typique et contemporain correspondant à l'image de marque de l'entreprise. Avec pour résultat un édifice compact faisant un large usage non seulement du verre, mais aussi du bois — ce qui renvoie au secteur d'activité de Rothoblaas.

Counter in lobby. Theke am Empfang. Comptoir de l'accueil.

From left to right, from above to below:
Conference room, staircase, workspace, office.
Right: View from lobby toward landscape.

Von links nach rechts, von oben nach unten:
Tagungsraum, Treppe, Arbeitsplatz, Büro.
Rechts: Blick von Lobby in Richtung Landschaft.

De gauche à droite, de haut en bas:
Salle de conférence, escalier, espace de travail, bureau.
Droite: Vue du hall sur l'extérieur.

# MONOVOLUME

www.monovolume.cc
**Client:** Blaas OHG, **Completion:** 2007, **Gross floor area:** 1,250 m², **Photos:** Oskar Da Riz, Bozen.

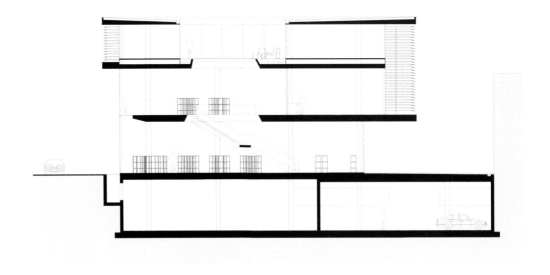

Left: South façade. Links: Südfassade. Gauche: Façade sud. | Right: Section. Rechts: Schnitt. Droite: Coupe.

The building with a full glass façade extending across two floors resembles a showcase. A balcony extending approximately five meters serves as a canopy for the customer entrance and also as an employee outdoor area for special workshop activities. The entrance area features an inviting free standing stairway with an organic stairway opening and a skylight above. This skylight allows excellent two-sided illumination of the office work places. The massive construction style provides enough thermal mass to allow the building to absorb heat during the day and to release it during the night.

Das Gebäude mit seiner über zwei Geschosse durchsichtigen Ganzglasfassade gleicht einer Vitrine. Ein rund fünf Meter auskragender Balkon dient dem Kundeneingang als Vordach und zugleich den Mitarbeitern als Außenbereich für spezielle Werkstattarbeiten. Im Eingangsbereich befindet sich die einladende, frei eingeschobene Treppe mit dem organischen Treppenloch und dem darüberliegenden Oberlicht. Dieses Oberlicht ermöglicht eine hervorragende zweiseitige Belichtung der Büroarbeitsplätze. Die Massivbauweise stellt genügend Speichermasse zur Verfügung, über die das Bauwerk tagsüber Wärme aufnehmen und nachts wieder abgeben kann.

Une façade en verre sur deux étages confère à ce bâtiment l'aspect d'une vitrine. Le balcon de cinq mètres de long qui s'étire au-dessus de l'entrée peut être utilisé pour certains travaux devant être réalisés à l'extérieur. Au centre du hall d'entrée se trouve un grand escalier surmonté d'une verrière qui contribue au bon éclairage naturel des bureaux, ainsi éclairés de deux côtés à la fois. Une construction massive permet au bâtiment d'emmagasiner la chaleur durant la journée, pour la restituer durant les heures froides.

Showroom. Verkaufsraum. Lieu d'exposition.

From left to right, from above to below:
Concrete façade, skylight, workspaces.
Right: Roof garden.

Von links nach rechts, von oben nach unten:
Betonfassade, Oberlicht, Arbeitsräume.
Rechts: Dachgarten.

De gauche à droite, de haut en bas:
Façade en béton, lucarne, espaces de travail.
Droite: Terrasse sur le toit.

# NPC ARCHITECTURE GROUP

www.npc-arq.com.br

**Client:** Young & Rubicam, **Completion:** 2004, **Gross floor area:** 2,000 m², **Photos:** Nelson Kon.

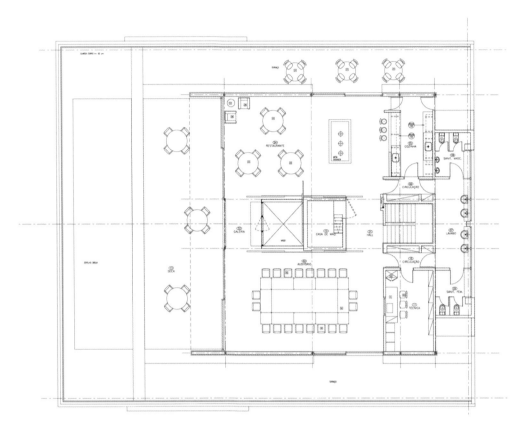

Left: **Entrance view**. Links: Blick auf den Eingang. Gauche: Vue sur l'entrée. | **Right: First floor plan**. Rechts: Grundriss erste Etage. Droite: Plan du 1er étage.

In a region undergoing great transformation, an abandoned building was invaded and looted. The architects freed selected structural lines of the building with the strategy to clean and reveal. The introduction of translucent, colorful glass volumes places inside and on the terrace and interconnected vertically through a central slit lights up the interior. Glass volumes cross the building vertically and bring natural light into the central square, allowing the integration of all floors. A red volume crosses the building, creating a 12 meter-high space that accommodates the central square for public activities.

In einer von tiefgreifenden Veränderungen geprägten Region wurde ein verlassenes Haus aufgebrochen und geplündert. Um es zu entkernen und zu exponieren, legten die Architekten ausgewählte Baulinien frei. Innen und auf der Terrasse eingefügte transluzente farbige Glasvolumen sind vertikal durch einen zentralen Schlitz miteinander verbunden und hellen den Innenraum auf. Glasvolumen queren den Raum vertikal. Sie bringen natürliches Licht in den zentralen Hof, sodass alle Ebenen von ihm profitieren. Ein rotes Volumen kreuzt den Bau und schafft einen 12 Meter hohen Raum mit dem zentralen Hof für die öffentlichen Aktivitäten.

Cet immeuble situé dans une région en pleine mutation a été laissé à l'abandon et pillé. Les architectes l'ont réhabilité en suivant une stratégie clairement définie. Des espaces en verre translucides et colorés ont été aménagés afin d'optimiser l'éclairage naturel de l'intérieur. Reliés verticalement les uns aux autres, ces espaces contribuent par ailleurs à l'intégration des différents étages. Au cœur du bâtiment se trouve un volume rouge de douze mètres de haut destiné aux manifestations publiques.

From left to right, from above to below:
Open workspaces, view on ground floor,
interior ground floor, atrium.
Right: General view.

Von links nach rechts, von oben nach unten:
Offene Bürolandschaft, Blick auf das Erdgeschoss,
Innenansicht Erdgeschoss, Atrium.
Rechts: Außenansicht.

De gauche à droite, de haut en bas:
Espaces libres de travail, vue sur le rez-de-chaussée,
vue du rez-de-chaussée, atrium.
Droite: Vue d'ensemble

# SAGA NEW OFFICE BUILDING,
## HAMBURG, GERMANY

PETER SIGL
NPS TCHOBAN VOSS ARCHITEKTEN
A.M. PRASCH, S. TCHOBAN, E. VOSS

www.npstv.de
Client: SAGA – Erste Immobiliengesellschaft mbH / SpriAG Sprinkenhof AG, Hamburg, Completion: 2004,
Gross floor area: 15,400 m², Photos: Klemens Ortmeyer.

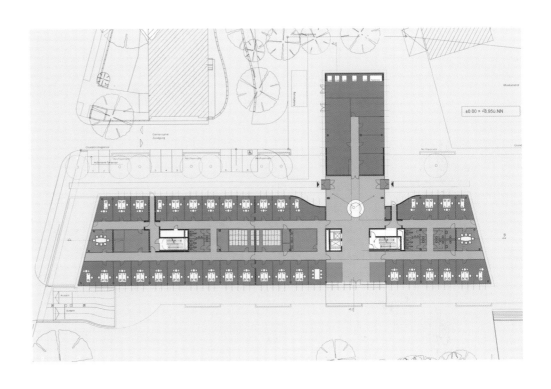

Left: Entrance hall. Links: Eingangshalle. Gauche: Hall d'entrée. | Right: Ground floor plan. Rechts: Grundriss Erdgeschoss. Droite: Plan du rez-de-chaussée.

The administrative building design follows the urban concept of linear stacking. The cubical volume consists of an oblong bar-shaped building, whose eastern contour delineates the museum's yard, spatially interacting with it. The cube develops from the inside out, housing about 400 offices in a tripartite structure with five stories and penthouse. The north wing adjoins the building with its five stories. A reaction to the existing landscape is created by adding "windows to the channel" – completely glazed, playfully arranged conference room boxes along the façade.

Der Entwurf des Verwaltungsgebäudes folgt dem städtebaulichen Prinzip der linearen Staffelung. Der Kubus besteht aus einem länglichen Gebäuderiegel, dessen östliche Begrenzung auf dem Museumshof endet und diesen dadurch räumlich fasst. Der Bau entwickelt sich von innen nach außen und nimmt Büros für circa 400 Mitarbeiter als dreibündige Anlage in fünf Geschossen und einem Staffelgeschoss auf. Im Norden schließt ein zweibündiger Gebäudeteil mit ebenfalls fünf Etagen an. Eine Reaktion auf die Landschaft sind zusätzliche „Fenster zum Kanal" – vollständig verglaste, spielerisch angeordnete Quader mit Konferenzräume die bei Dunkelheit illuminiert werden.

Cet immeuble administratif s'inscrit dans un concept d'urbanisme linéaire. Il se compose d'une barre bordée à l'est par la cour du musée voisin. Ce volume cubique complété par une extension latérale abrite quelque quatre cents bureaux répartis sur cinq étages. Une salle de conférence entièrement vitrée caractérisée par une sobre décoration s'ouvre largement sur le paysage environnant.

Conference room. Sitzungssaal. Salle de conférence.

From left to right, from above to below:
Atirum, detail atrium, guidance system, hallway.
Right: Conference room.

Von links nach rechts, von oben nach unten:
Atrium, Detail Atrium, Leitsystem, Flur.
Rechts: Tagungsraum.

De gauche à droite, de haut en bas:
Atrium, détail de l'atrium, système de repérage, couloir.
Droite: Salle de conférence.

SERGEI TSCHOBAN
NPS TCHOBAN VOSS ARCHITEKTEN
A.M. PRASCH, S. TCHOBAN, E. VOSS

www.npstv.de

**Client:** 1. Bauwert Portfolio Gamma GmbH, 2. (from implementation planing) Müller-Altvatter Bauunternehmung GmbH & Co. KG, **Completion:** 2006, **Gross floor area:** 27,500 m², **Photos:** Claus Graubner.

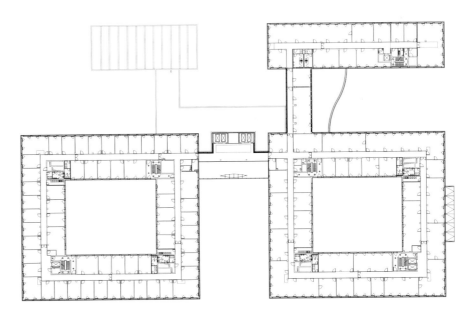

Left: Main entrance. Links: Haupteingang. Gauche: Entrée principale. | Right: Typical floor plan. Rechts: Regelgeschossplan. Droite: Plan caractéristique.

The six-story administration building describes with its ground figure a structure system of four basic parts, connected through binding elements, such as the veins of a toothed leaf. It is made accessible by a centrally located main entrance area. This area simultaneously works as both horizontal and vertical opening and connecting passage for the two main buildings (with exclusive office use) and the rear smaller flank buildings. The contemporary façades contain a generous glazed portion allowing an optimal natural illumination of the office areas. The closed sections of the perforated façade consist of glass panels with motive-based imprints.

Das sechsgeschossige Verwaltungsgebäude beschreibt mit seiner Grundform im Wesentlichen vier Einzelbaukörper. Als Bindeglied zwischen ihnen dienen Verbindungsbauten ähnlich den Adern eines gezackten Blattes. Erschlossen wird das Ensemble über einen zentral platzierten Haupteingangsbereich. Diese Zone fungiert gleichzeitig als horizontaler und vertikaler Übergang zu den beiden Hauptgebäuden (mit ausschließlicher Büronutzung) und den rückseitigen kleineren Bauten. Die modernen Fassaden gewähren mit ihren großzügigen Glasanteilen eine optimale natürliche Belichtung der Büroflächen. Die geschlossenen Fassadenabschnitte sind mit ornamental bedrucktem Glas verkleidet.

Cet immeuble de bureaux de six étages se compose de quatre volumes de base reliés entre eux, avec un plan qui rappelle une feuille dentée. L'accès se fait par un hall central qui dessert les deux volumes principaux horizontalement et verticalement, ainsi que les deux volumes auxiliaires situés sur la face arrière de l'ensemble. Les façades sont largement vitrées de manière à optimiser l'éclairage naturel des bureaux. Les espaces opaques de la façade se composent de panneaux de verres décorés.

From left to right, from above to below:
Conference room, hallway, general view.
Right: Entrance view toward elevators.

Von links nach rechts, von oben nach unten:
Tagungsraum, Flur, Gesamtansicht.
Rechts: Eingang mit Blick in Richtung Fahrstühle.

De gauche à droite, de haut en bas:
Salle de conférence, couloir, vue générale.
Droite: Entrée avec vue sur les ascenseurs.

# LAW FIRM HENGELER MUELLER CORPORATE INTERIOR DESIGN,
## DÜSSELDORF, GERMANY

# THOMAS PINK |
# PETZINKA PINK ARCHITECTS

www.technologische-architektur.de
**Client:** Law firm Hengeler Mueller, **Completion:** 2003, **Gross floor area:** 15,000 m², **Photos:** Tomas Riehle, Cologne.

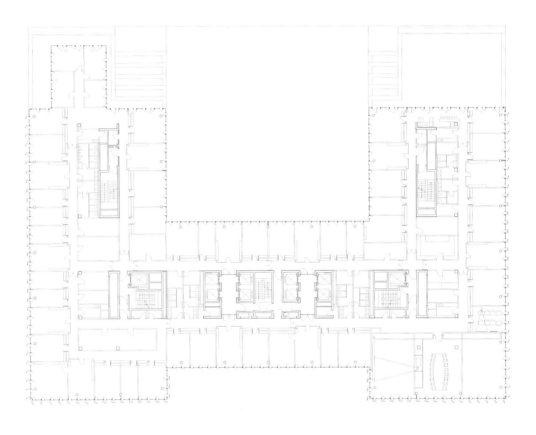

Left: Lobby. Links: Empfang. Gauche: Accueil. | Right: Seventh floor plan. Rechts: Grundriss siebte Etage. Droite: Plan du 7e étage.

In the heart of Düsseldorf's banking district, the firm Thomas Pink | Petzinka Pink Architects designed a new corporate interior for one of Europes most successful law firms. Over a total of 15,000 m² of floor space a stringent spatial concept, the futuristic technological facilities and the consistent design of all the fittings and furniture created a harmonious overall impression and a distinguished appearance. The subtle, timeless elegance of wood, stone, stainless steel, and glass, the perfect craftsmanship and consistency in the organization of space are the hallmarks of this impressive example of interior design customized to suit the requirements of a major European law firm.

Mitten im Düsseldorfer Bankenviertel entwarf Thomas Pink | Petzinka Pink eine neue Innenarchitektur für eine der renommiertesten Anwaltskanzleien Europas. Auf einer Fläche von insgesamt 15.000 m² entstand durch ein strenges Raumkonzept, futuristische Technik und das konsequente Design von Ausstattung und Mobiliar ein harmonischer Gesamteindruck und ein bemerkenswertes Erscheinungsbild. Die subtile, zeitlose Eleganz von Holz, Stein, Edelstahl und Glas, das vollendete handwerkliche Können und die Stringenz in der räumlichen Organisation kennzeichnen dieses eindrucksvolle Beispiel einer auf die Bedürfnisse einer der bedeutendsten europäischen Anwaltssozietät abgestimmten Raumgestaltung.

Les architectes ont réaménagé l'intérieur de cet immeuble situé au cœur du quartier des affaires de Düsseldorf à la demande d'un des principaux cabinets d'avocats européens. Sur une superficie de quinze mille mètres carrés, un concept spatial rigoureux utilise des équipements et des meubles futuristes pour créer une atmosphère à la fois harmonieuse et distinguée. Les aménagements intérieurs se caractérisent par une organisation stricte et par l'élégance subtile et intemporelle de matériaux tels le bois, la pierre, le verre et l'inox, mis en œuvre d'une manière qui touche à la perfection.

KONFERENZRAUM

From left to right, from above to below:
Office bar, hallway light stela,
sideboard, guidance system.
Right: Conference room.

Von links nach rechts, von oben nach unten:
Bürobar, Flur mit Lichtstele,
Anrichte, Leitsystem.
Rechts: Tagungsraum.

De gauche à droite, de haut en bas:
Bar, couloir avec installations lumineuses,
buffet, système de repérage.
Droite: Salle de conférence.

# LBS HEADQUARTERS,
## HANOVER, GERMANY

# ARCHITECTS – ENGINEERS PSP

www.architekten-psp.de
Client: LBS-Norddeutsche Landesbausparkasse, Completion: 2002, Gross floor area: 26,736 m², Photos: Klemens Ortmeyer.

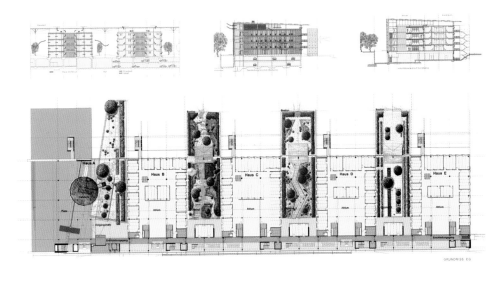

Left: Façade with planted courtyard. Links: Fassade mit bepflanztem Innenhof vom Park. Gauche: Façade avec cour gazonnée. | Right: Ground floor plan, sections. Rechts: Erdgeschossplan, Schnitte. Droite: Plan du rez-chaussée, coupe.

The office building is distinguished by a continuous glass roof measuring 175 x 40 meter and a similarly long approximately 18 meter high glass wall. Beneath this glass angle, four identical four-story "houses" are arranged with a decentralized engineering room between the glass roof and the last floor. A narrower head building contains the administration, conference and visitor consultation areas, as well as a bistro. The "green yards" between the buildings are closed off by a glass wall that can be opened in the summer and that feature different gardening design styles. This makes it possible to abstain from heating the offices.

Charakteristisch für das Bürogebäude ist ein durchgängiges 175 x 40 Meter großes Glasdach und eine ebenso lange 18 Meter hohen Glaswand zur Hauptstraße. Unter diesem Glaswinkel sind vier baugleiche viergeschossige „Häuser" mit Kombibüros, jeweils dezentral über eine Technikzentrale zwischen Glasdach und letztem Geschoss versorgt, angeordnet, dazu als Kopfbau ein schmaleres Haus mit den Sonderfunktionen Vorstand, Konferenz, Besucherberatung und Bistro. Die „Grünhöfe" zwischen den Häusern sind mit einer im Sommer komplett zu öffnenden Glaswand zum Außenraum abgeschlossen und unterschiedlich gartenarchitektonisch gestaltet. Sie ermöglichen außerdem den Verzicht auf das Heizen der Büros.

Cet immeuble de bureaux se caractérise par un toit entièrement en verre de 175 mètres par quarante et un pan de façade également en verre d'environ dix-huit mètres de haut. Sous le toit commun se trouvent quatre édifices distincts de quatre étages chacun, ainsi qu'un bâtiment situé à une extrémité de l'ensemble qui abrite un café, l'accueil des visiteurs, une salle de conférence et les bureaux de la direction. Un local situé entre le dernier étage et le toit en verre rassemble tous les équipements techniques alimentant les différents bâtiments. Les espaces verts aménagés à l'intérieur du complexe sont fermés par une paroi en verre entièrement amovible.

From left to right, from above to below:
Detail planted courtyard, bridge in entrance hall,
typical office, stairway.
Right: Main entrance free area.

Von links nach rechts, von oben nach unten:
Detail im bepflanzten Innenhof, Brücke in Eingangshalle,
typisches Büro, Treppe.
Rechts: Haupteingang Vorplatz.

De gauche à droite, de haut en bas:
Détail du jardin intérieur, rampe dans le hall d'entrée,
espace de travail, escalier.
Droite: Entrée principale préplace.

# CLICK 3X LA,
## LOS ANGELES, CA, USA

# PUGH + SCARPA ARCHITECTS

www.pugh-scarpa.com
Client: Click 3X LA, Completion: 1998, Gross floor area: 836 m², Photos: Marvin Rand.

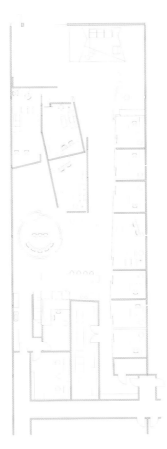

Left: Entrance view. Links: Blick auf den Eingang. Gauche: Vue de l'entrée. | Right: Floor plan. Rechts: Grundriss. Droite: Plan.

The design for Click 3X LA transforms an industrial wasteland into a dramatic setting for a digital effects and animation studio. Located at Bergamot Station, the internationally known art center, this renovation and expansion involved adding 2,500 square feet to an existing 6,500 square feet industrial building formerly used to manufacture residential water heaters. The dense, technologically-rich program includes Inferno rooms used to create visual effects and computer animation for TV commercials and shows and large-format movies. Also included are several other computer animation studios, AVID rooms, CGI suites, open production space, conference rooms, executive offices and a machine room.

Der Entwurf für Click 3X LA macht aus einem industriellen Ödland das spannungsreiche Umfeld eines Studios für digitale Effekte und Animation. Das an der Bergamot Station, einem international bekannten Kunstzentrum, gelegene Projekt umfasst den Umbau und die Erweiterung eines bestehenden Fabrikgebäudes. Das kompakte, technologisch anspruchsvolle Programm beinhaltet Inferno-Räume, in denen visuelle Effekte und Computeranimationen für TV-Werbespots und TV-Shows erzeugt und Großbildfilme hergestellt werden. Dazu gehören auch mehrere Studios für Computeranimation, AVID-Räume, CGI-Trakte, offene Produktionsbereiche, Konferenzräume, Chefbüros und ein Technikraum.

Cet immeuble est situé à Bergamot Station, le plus grand centre culturel du sud de la Californie. Le projet portait sur la conversion d'un ancien bâtiment industriel et la construction de nouveaux locaux afin de faire passer la surface totale d'environ 2000 mètres carrés plus de 2800 mètres carrés. La salle high-tech nouvellement créée permet de réaliser des effets spéciaux et des animations numériques pour les spots publicitaires, les spectacles et le cinéma. L'immeuble abrite également d'autres studios d'animation, ainsi que des bureaux, des salles AVID, des suites CGI, des espaces de production ouverts, des salles de conférence et une salle des machines.

From left to right, from above to below:
Conference room, lobby, office construction.
Right: Detail construction.

Von links nach rechts, von oben nach unten:
Tagungsraum, Empfang, Bürokonstruktion.
Rechts: Konstruktionsdetail.

De gauche à droite, de haut en bas:
Salle de conférence, mansarde, construction de bureau.
Droite: Détail de construction.

# OFFICE AND COMMERCIAL BUILDING IN FALKENRIED,
## HAMBURG, GERMANY

# RENNER HAINKE WIRTH

www.rhwarchitekten.de

**Client:** STRABAG Projektentwicklung GmbH, **Completion:** 2007, **Gross floor area:** 17,600 m², **Photos:** Uwe Scholz.

Left: Exterior view. Links: Außenansicht. Gauche: Vue extérieure. | **Right:** Ground floor plan. Rechts: Grundriss Erdgeschoss. Droite: Plan du rez-de-chaussée.

The building is a bold expansion of a typical specimen of "box" architecture from the 1970s in Hamburg's ambitious Falkenried district. It owes its red color to its Falkenried neighbors, which consist largely of old brick factory buildings, where streetcars were once built and maintained, and new brick townhouses. This mundane, functional structure also marks the transition to a main exit road dating to the 1950s. To give it a more noble appearance, the architects have resorted to a trick: the added floors have been designed in the form of a floating "Wolkenbügel" a kind of horizontal skyscraper. A compelling use of color is also evident in the interior.

Das Gebäude ist eine kühne Erweiterung einer typischen „Kasten"-Architektur aus den 1970er Jahren in Hamburgs aufstrebendem Quartier Falkenried. Seine rote Farbe verdankt es den benachbarten alten Backsteinbauten, in denen früher Straßenbahnen hergestellt und gewartet wurden, sowie den neuen Stadthäusern aus Ziegelstein. Diese nüchterne funktionelle Konstruktion markiert auch den Übergang zu einer Ausfallstraße aus den 1950er Jahren. Damit sie stattlicher wirkt, wandten die Architekten einen Kunstgriff an: Die ergänzten Geschosse sind in Form eines schwebenden „Wolkenbügels" gestaltet, einer Art horizontalem Hochhaus. Eine reizvolle Farbgebung zeigt sich auch in den Innenräumen.

Une « boîte » typique de l'architecture des années 1970, construite à Hambourg-Falkenried, a été récemment réaménagée de manière audacieuse. Le revêtement rouge de la façade reprend la couleur des nombreux bâtiments en briques, tant industriels que résidentiels, construits autrefois dans ce quartier ouvrier réaménagé une première fois dans les années 1950. Les architectes ont utilisé une astuce pour donner au bâtiment une apparence plus noble, voire mondaine : ils ont surélevé l'édifice existant à l'aide d'une sorte de « gratte-ciel horizontal » qui semble flotter sur le bâtiment d'origine. Les nouveaux aménagements intérieurs font eux aussi un usage rigoureux de la couleur.

From left to right, from above to below:
Façade, loft, brick façade
Right: Street side view.

Von links nach rechts, von oben nach unten:
Fassade, Dachgeschoss, Backsteinfassade.
Rechts: Blick von der Straße.

De gauche à droite, de haut en bas:
Façade, loft, façade en briques.
Droite: Vue depuis la rue.

# LARCHMONT OFFICE,
## LOS ANGELES, CA, USA

# RIOS CLEMENTI HALE STUDIOS

www.rchstudios.com

**Client:** Rios Clementi Hale Studios, **Completion:** 2008, **Gross floor area:** 1,579 m², **Photos:** Tom Bonner, Santa Monica (218, 220 a.l., 220 a.r., 220 b.r., 221), Rios Clementi Hale Studios, Los Angeles (220 b.l.).

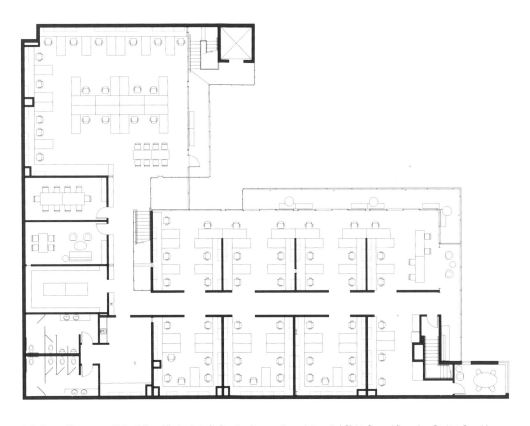

Left: Open office spaces. Links: Offene Bürolandschaft. Gauche: Espaces libres de travail. | Right: Second floor plan. Rechts: Grundriss zweite Etage. Droite: Plan du 2e étage.

Rios Clementi Hale Studios renovated a former mini-mall for its multi-disciplined design staff. Replacing exterior walls with window wall systems created screened porches around the second-floor studio space. Exterior panels alternate between mirrored glass and expressive cut aluminum screens. A display wall along the staircase exhibits photos, boards, and models of past, current, and future architecture projects of the firm. A nonhierarchical studio environment exists in pod work groups of six or 19. The "tree house" meeting room features floor-to-ceiling windows overlooking the street trees.

Rios Clementi Hale Studios bauten für ihr multidisziplinäres Designteam ein ehemaliges Mini-Einkaufszentrum um. Sie ersetzten Außenmauern durch Wandsysteme mit Fenstern und schufen so geschützte Veranden um den Studiobereich im zweiten Geschoss. Die Außenplatten bestehen abwechselnd aus Spiegelglas und ausdrucksvoll geschnittenen Aluminiumabschirmungen. Auf einer Schauwand entlang der Treppe sind frühere, aktuelle und zukünftige Architekturprojekte des Studios zu sehen. Die nicht hierarchisch organisierte Büroumgebung enthält Arbeitseinheiten für sechs bis neunzehn Mitarbeiter. Im Besprechungszimmer „Baumhaus" gewährt ein raumhohes Fenster Ausblicke auf die Straßenbäume.

Le bureau d'architectes Rios Clementi Hale Studios s'est installé dans une ancienne galerie marchande qu'il avait lui-même reconvertie. Les murs du second niveau ont été remplacés par des baies vitrées afin d'optimiser l'éclairage naturel des postes de travail. Sur la façade, des miroirs alternent avec des panneaux d'aluminium décorés de manière expressive. Des photos des réalisations passées et futures de l'entreprise sont exposées dans l'escalier. Les employés travaillent par groupes de six à dix-neuf selon une hiérarchie plate. La salle de réunion baptisée « Tree House » est entièrement vitrée du sol au plafond et domine les arbres de la rue.

From left to right, from above to below:
Exterior view, long walls as pin-up space,
conference room, workstations.
Right: Shop at entrance hall.

Von links nach rechts, von oben nach unten:
Außenansicht, lange Wände dienen als Pinnwand,
Besprechungsraum, Arbeitsplätze.
Rechts: Geschäft in der Eingangshalle.

De gauche à droite, de haut en bas:
Vue extérieure, long mur avec affiches,
salle de conférence, espaces de travail.
Droite: Magasin dans le hall d'entrée.

# KROMANN REUMERT DOMICILE,
## COPENHAGEN, DENMARK

# SCHMIDT HAMMER LASSEN ARCHITECTS

www.shl.dk

Client: PFA Pension A/S, Completion: 2002, Gross floor area: 14,000 m², Photos: Jørgen True.

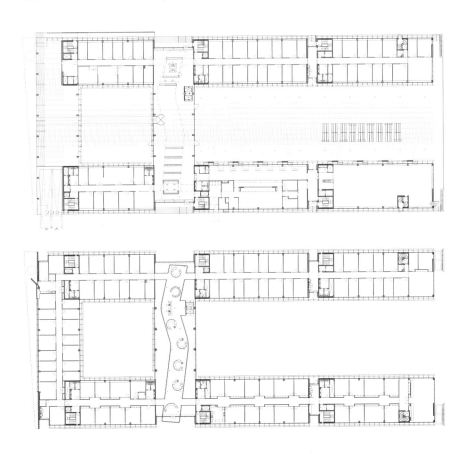

Left: Interior with balconies. Links: Inneneinrichtung mit Balkonen. Gauche: Intérieur avec balcons. | Right: Fourth floor plan. Rechts: Grundriss vierte Etage. Droite: Plan du 4e étage.

The building presents itself as a distinctively monolithic piece of architecture, well-geared to frame a specific working environment. The compactness and elegant austerity of the main façade facing the city is relieved by a friendly canopy-sheltered flight of steps that leads through to an atrium and on into the foyer. The offices are positioned so as to allow visual contact both to the foyer and the courtyard, while offering views out towards the extensive docks. The common functional areas cluster around a vertical indoor plaza on four levels. Three curved hanging balconies contain the main reception, mailroom, library, lounge and customer reception facilities.

Die ausgeprägt monolithische Architektur des Gebäudes bietet einen geeigneten Rahmen für die spezielle Arbeitsumgebung. Eine einladende überdachte Treppe mildert die Kompaktheit und elegante Strenge der Hauptfassade zur Stadt hin. Sie führt zu einem Atrium und in das Foyer. Die Anordnung der Büros gestattet den Sichtkontakt zum Foyer sowie zum Innenhof und gewährt Aussichten auf die weitläufigen Hafenanlagen. Die gemeinschaftlichen Funktionsbereiche gruppieren sich um eine viergeschossige Plaza. Drei geschwungene abgehängte Balkons enthalten Empfang, Poststelle, Bibliothek, Sitzecken und Kundenzonen.

Ce bâtiment d'aspect monolithique offre tous les avantages d'un environnement de travail spécifique. L'escalier couvert qui mène à la verrière du hall d'entrée s'intègre à la façade principale, à la fois compacte et d'une élégante austérité. Les bureaux sont disposés de manière à offrir des vues sur le hall, la cour intérieure ou les docks voisins. Les espaces fonctionnels se regroupent sur quatre niveaux autour d'un espace ouvert situé à l'intérieur du bâtiment. Des galeries aux formes incurvées accueillent le foyer, la bibliothèque, la salle du courrier et la réception des clients.

From left to right, from above to below:
Detail garden, library, conference room, balcony.
Right: Meeting area.

Von links nach rechts, von oben nach unten:
Gartendetail, Bibliothek, Tagungsraum, Balkon.
Rechts: Aufenthaltsraum.

De gauche à droite, de haut en bas:
Détail du jardin, bibliothèque, salle de conférence, balcon.
Droite: Salle de rencontres.

# UNIVERSAL MUSIC GROUP,
## BERLIN, GERMANY

# SEHW ARCHITECTS

www.sehw.de

**Client:** Universal Music Group, **Completion:** 2003, **Gross floor area:** 3,900 m², **Photos:** Jürgen Schmidt.

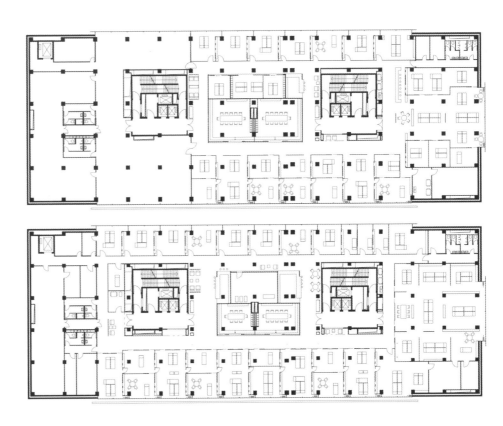

Left: Cafeteria. Links: Cafeteria. Gauche: Cafétéria. | Right: Third and fourth floor plan. Rechts: Grundriss dritte und vierte Etage. Droite: Plans des 3e et 4e étages.

To allow daylight to penetrate as far as possible inside the 35-meter deep building, two consecutive office areas in the southern part were designed exclusively with glass separation walls parallel to the façade. Light-colored materials were used for the floors to reflect the daylight to the inside. The diagonal division is achieved by massive shelves with sliding elements of stained oak and doors that provide an additional longitudinal connection. The transparent system of glass and cupboard elements creates the impression of an open-plan, while providing the privacy of smaller room units.

Um bei der Gebäudetiefe von 35 Metern das Tageslicht soweit wie möglich in das Gebäudeinnere zu führen, wurden im südlichen Teil zwei hintereinander liegende Bürozonen ausschließlich mit Glastrennwänden parallel zur Fassade geplant. Für die Böden wurden helle Materialien verwendet, um das Tageslicht nach Innen zu reflektieren. Die Unterteilung in Querrichtung erfolgt durch massive Regale mit Schiebeelementen aus gebeizter Eiche und Türen, die einen weiteren Verbindungsweg in Längsrichtung ermöglichen. Das transparente System aus Glas- und Schrankelementen schafft den Eindruck eines Großraumbüros, gewährleistet jedoch die Intimität kleinerer Raumeinheiten.

Afin d'optimiser l'éclairage naturel à l'intérieur de cet immeuble d'une profondeur totale de trente-cinq mètres, les architectes ont aménagé deux zones de bureaux séparées par une cloison en verre le long de la façade sud. Ils ont également choisi un matériau clair pour le revêtement de sol afin de favoriser la réflexion de la lumière. Perpendiculairement à ces deux rangées de bureaux se dressent des placards coulissant en chêne massif, tandis que des portes assurent la communication dans le sens transversal. Les cloisons en verre donnent aux employés l'impression de travailler dans un bureau collectif, tout en préservant une certaine intimité.

Conference room "box". Tagungsraum „box". Salle de conférence „box".

From left to right, from above to below:
Bar, counter of stained oak,
workspaces, interior.
Right: Conference room.

Von links nach rechts, von oben nach unten:
Bar, Theke aus gebeizter Eiche,
Arbeitsräume, Inneneinrichtung.
Rechts: Tagungsraum.

De gauche à droite, de haut en bas:
Bar, comptoir en chêne verni,
espaces de travail, intérieur.
Droite: Salle de conférence.

# HYDRAULX,
## SANTA MONICA, CA, USA

## SHUBIN + DONALDSON ARCHITECTS

www.shubinanddonaldson.com
**Client:** Hydraulx, **Completion:** 2007, **Gross floor area:** 1,393 m², **Photos:** Tom Bonner, Santa Monica.

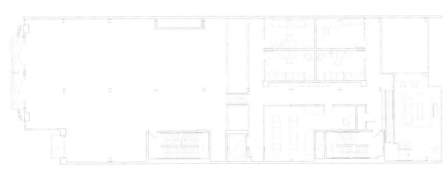

Left: Client lounge. Links: Kundenlounge. Gauche: Espace d'accueil pour les clients. | **Right:** Floor plans. Rechts: Grundrisse. Droite: Plans.

Shubin + Donaldson Architects designed a four-level office with flexibility to keep up with constant changes in the client's industry. Space planning was crucial to provide both private and collaborative environments. The architecture expresses the operation of the machine. The material truth of exposed structure and raw industrial materials defines the palette. Glass, steel, aluminum, perforated metal, acrylic plastic, and clear-coated MDF are joined with exposed details. Custom-designed workstations are powered by intense overhead cable threading through the space. The glass-walled Machine Room – the brain of operations – houses powerful computers that serve sophisticated workstations.

Um den ständigen Veränderungen in der Branche des Kunden gerecht zu werden, gestalteten Shubin + Donaldson Architects ein viergeschossiges Büro sehr flexibel. Beim Entwurf der Einzel- und Teamarbeitsplätze war die Raumplanung wesentlich. Das exponierte Tragwerk und die roh belassenen industriellen Werkstoffe bestimmen die Materialpalette. Glas, Stahl, Aluminium, Acrylglas und klarlackbehandelte MDF-Platten sind sichtbar miteinander verbunden. Die Arbeitsplätze werden von einem hoch liegenden Kabel versorgt, das sich durch den Raum zieht. In dem von Glaswänden umschlossenen „Maschinenraum" stehen leistungsstarke Computer, die hochentwickelte Arbeitsplätze versorgen.

Cet immeuble sur quatre niveaux a été conçu pour s'adapter à l'évolution constante de l'utilisateur. Les architectes ont développé des espaces individuels et des zones de collaboration en élaborant un bâtiment qui fonctionne comme une machine. Les divers matériaux utilisés – verre, acier, aluminium, acrylique, métal perforé et plaques MDF – ont été laissés bruts et font apparaître les détails des surfaces. Les postes de travail personnalisés sont desservis par tout un ensemble de câbles et conduits accrochés au plafond. La « salle des machines » – le centre opérationnel de l'entreprise – abrite de puissants ordinateurs reliés à des postes individuels sophistiqués.

From left to right, from above to below:
View to library, multi-level workspaces,
employee kitchen, view torward machine room.
Right: Spaces for group work.

Von links nach rechts, von oben nach unten:
Blick in die Bibliothek, Arbeitsräume auf mehreren Ebenen,
Mitarbeiterküche, Blick in Richtung Maschinenraum.
Rechts: Räume für Gruppenarbeit.

De gauche à droite, de haut en bas:
Vue sur la librairie, espaces de travail sur plusieurs niveaux,
cuisine des employés, vue sur la salle des machines.
Droite: Espace de travail pour groupe.

## SHUBIN + DONALDSON ARCHITECTS

www.shubinanddonaldson.com

**Client:** Ogilvy Los Angeles, **Completion:** 2000, **Gross floor area:** 2,787 m², **Photos:** Tom Bonner, Santa Monica.

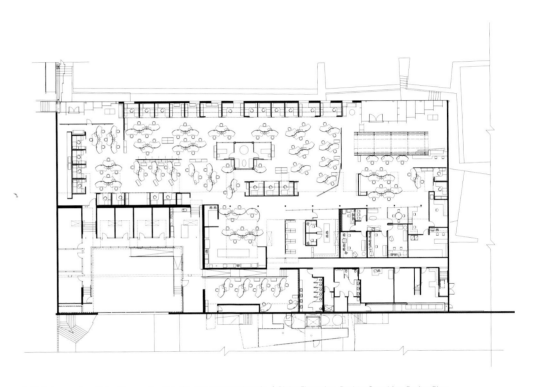

Left: Entrance view. Links: Eingangsbereich. Gauche: Vue sur l'entrée. | Right: Floor plan. Rechts: Grundriss. Droite: Plan.

The office communicates a commitment to cutting-edge work by the international ad agency, which selected Shubin + Donaldson Architects to revamp its image through the workplace. Behind an angled plate-glass wall, a perforated metal tunnel known as "The Tube" dominates the entrance and serves as a gallery entry path to the rest of the building. The 14-foot-high, steel-framed structure skinned with perforated aluminum sheets holds display screens. Custom-designed workstations use the same materials seen throughout the space – perforated metal and steel – to construct a strong integration between the building and its function.

Das Büro veranschaulicht die Verpflichtung der internationalen Werbeagentur zu innovativer Arbeit. Shubin + Donaldson Architects sollten über den Arbeitsplatz das Image der Firma aufbessern. Hinter einer Glaswand beherrscht ein perforierter Metalltunnel den Eingang – „The Tube". Er führt in das Innere des Gebäudes und dient mit seinen Bildschirmen als Galerie. Diese 4,27 Meter hohe Stahlrahmenkonstruktion ist mit perforierten Aluminiumtafeln bedeckt. Bei den kundenspezifischen Arbeitsstationen finden sich die gleichen Materialien wie im gesamten Projekt – gelochtes Metall und Stahl –, wodurch eine enge Verbindung zwischen dem Gebäude und seiner Funktion entsteht.

Cet immeuble de bureaux manifeste l'esprit d'avant-garde de l'agence de publicité internationale qu'il abrite. Derrière une façade en verre, un tunnel en plaques d'aluminium perforées communément appelé « le tuyau » donne accès aux différents espaces intérieurs. Des écrans se trouvent dans cette structure de plus de quatre mètres de haut. L'acier et les plaques d'aluminium perforées se retrouvent dans les différents postes de travail personnalisés et contribuent ainsi à l'unité du bâtiment et de sa fonction.

From left to right, from above to below:
Glass enclosed main space, the "Tube",
workstations, offices in open space.
Right: Semi-enclosed office within workstation.

Von links nach rechts, von oben nach unten:
Verglaster zentraler Raum, die „Tube",
Arbeitsplätze, Arbeitsräume in offener Bürolandschaft.
Rechts: Halbgeschlossenes Büro innerhalb der Arbeitsplätze.

De gauche à droite, de haut en bas:
Espace central vitré, le „Tube",
bureaux de travail, espace de travail ouvert.
Droite: Bureau partiellent enfermè dans des postes de travail.

# SAATCHI + SAATCHI,
## CULVER CITY, CA, USA

# SHUBIN + DONALDSON ARCHITECTS

www.shubinanddonaldson.com

Client: Saatchi + Saatchi, Los Angeles, Completion: 2008, Gross floor area: 9,847 m², Photos: Tom Bonner, Santa Monica.

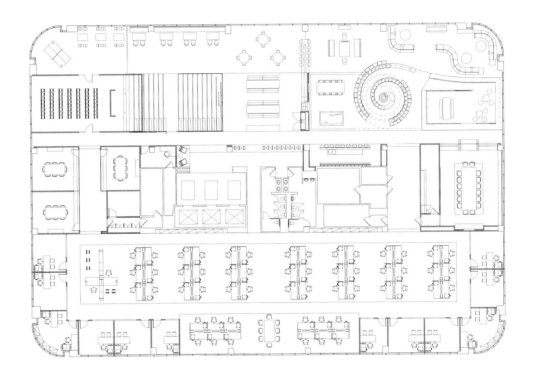

Left: Aluminum ceiling mimics stairway form. Links: Aluminiumdecke spiegelt die Treppe wider. Gauche: Plafond en aluminium se reflétant sur l'escalier. | Right: Third floor plan. Rechts: Grundriss dritte Etage. Droite: Plan du 3e étage.

Shubin + Donaldson Architects conceived Saatchi + Saatchi's design to incorporate concepts of "home". This mandate is fulfilled by a grand staircase / meeting space, living and dining areas, and a "backyard" for casual gathering. The centrally located main floor is highlighted by a communal hub to bring staff together to allow for impromptu collaborative moments. The theme of "homing at work" is apparent in a spiral library that imparts the concept of a hearth. The combination of seating and shelving offers employees a central area for reading, as well as a mini amphitheater for small inter-office presentations. The grand staircase serves dual purpose as connector and meeting area.

Shubin + Donaldson Architects bezogen beim Entwurf für Saatchi + Saatchi „häusliche" Konzepte ein. Dazu gehören eine Treppe / Begegnungszone, Wohn- und Essbereiche sowie ein „Hinterhof" für zwanglose Treffen. Das von einer Gemeinschafts-fläche betonte zentrale Hauptgeschoss soll die Beschäftigten zur Teamarbeit zusammenführen. Das Thema „Homing bei der Arbeit" veranschaulicht eine spiralförmige Bibliothek. Sie lässt an einen hei-mischen Herd denken. Die Kombination von Sitzgele-genheiten und Regalen bietet der Belegschaft einen Bereich zum Lesen sowie ein kleines Amphitheater für hausinterne Präsentationen. Die grandiose Trep-pe fungiert als Verbindung und als Begegnungszone.

Les architectes ont ici cherché à intégrer la notion de « chez soi » dans un immeuble de bureaux. C'est bien l'impression qui se dégage des gradins servant aux assemblées du personnel, ainsi que des salles à manger et de l' « arrière-cour » pour réunions informelles. Les employés peuvent aussi organiser des moments de collaboration impromptus dans l'espace central de l'entreprise. La notion de « chez soi » se retrouve dans la bibliothèque en spirale dont la forme rappelle un cœur. Les sièges et les étagères y sont propices à la lecture et aux présentations en comité restreint.

From left to right, from above to below:
Open seating and kitchen, meeting space,
main stairs, library.
Right: Spiral seating.

Von links nach rechts, von oben nach unten:
Offene Sitzgelegenheit und Küche, Aufenthaltsraum,
Haupttreppe, Bibliothek.
Rechts: Spiralförmige Sitzgelegenheit.

De gauche à droite, de haut en bas:
Places assises et espace cuisine ouvert,
salle de rencontre, escalier principal, bibliothèque.
Droite: Places assises en spirale.

# GLOBAL HYATT CORPORATE HEADQUARTERS,
## CHICAGO, IL, USA

SOM SKIDMORE, OWINGS &
MERRILL / STEPHEN APKING

www.som.com
**Client:** Higgins Development Partners and Hyatt Hotels Corporation, **Completion:** 2004, **Gross floor area:**
23,226 m², **Photos:** Jimmy Cohrsson.

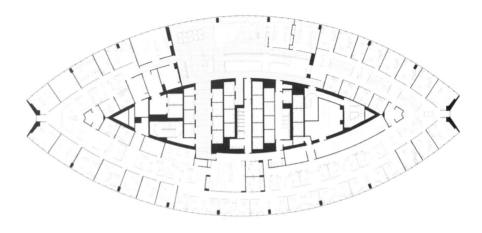

Left: Conference room. Links: Tagungsraum. Gauche: Salle de conférence. | Right: 12th floor plan. Rechts: Grundriss 12. Etage. Droite: Plan du 12e étage.

The global headquarters for Hyatt Hotels and the other Pritzker family businesses simultaneously represent a new forward-thinking work environment. The lobby of the building is treated almost like a hotel lobby. Because Hyatt invented the concept of the hotel atrium, SOM incorporated a multi-story atrium space that reinforces the company's core values and brand image, while also facilitating vertical communication between the different departments and company businesses. The liberal use of wood and other classic materials creates a Zen-like atmosphere that speaks directly to Hyatt's history of warm hospitality.

Die Weltzentrale für Hyatt Hotels und die anderen Geschäftsfelder der Pritzker-Familie repräsentiert eine neue vorausdenkende Gestaltung der Arbeitsumgebung. Die Lobby des Gebäudes gleicht nahezu einer Hotelhalle. Da das Konzept des Hotelatriums von Hyatt stammt, fügte SOM ein mehrgeschossiges Atrium ein. Dieses unterstreicht die grundlegenden Werte und das Markenimage des Unternehmens und erleichtert die vertikale Kommunikation zwischen einzelnen Abteilungen und Geschäftszweigen. Die großzügige Verwendung von Holz und anderen zeitlosen Materialien schafft eine Zen-ähnliche Atmosphäre, die Hyatts traditionelle Gastlichkeit bekundet.

Le siège social de Hyatt Hotels et des autres entreprises du groupe appartenant à la famille Pritzker se caractérise par un environnement de travail volontariste. Le hall d'entrée ressemble à une réception d'hôtel. Hyatt ayant été parmi les premières entreprises de l'industrie hôtelière à faire un large usage de la verrière, les architectes en ont évidemment inclut une à leur projet. Cette verrière, qui correspond ainsi à l'image de marque du client et abrite le hall d'entrée, donne accès aux différents étages du bâtiment. L'usage du bois et d'autres matériaux conventionnels crée une atmosphère zen qui renvoie directement à la tradition d'hospitalité de l'entreprise.

From left to right, from above to below:
Reception, private office, reception, staircase.
Right: Entrance hall.

Von links nach rechts, von oben nach unten:
Empfang, privates Büro, Empfang, Treppe.
Rechts: Eingangshalle.

De gauche à droite, de haut en bas:
Vue sur la réception, espace privé, réception, escalier.
Droite: Hall d'entrée.

# MAST-JÄGERMEISTER HEADQUARTERS,
## WOLFENBÜTTEL, GERMANY

## STRUHK ARCHITEKTEN
## PLANUNGSGSELLSCHAFT MBH

www.struhk.de
Client: Mast-Jägermeister AG, Wolfenbüttel, Completion: 2003, Gross floor area: 11,800 m², Photos: Jutta Brüdem.

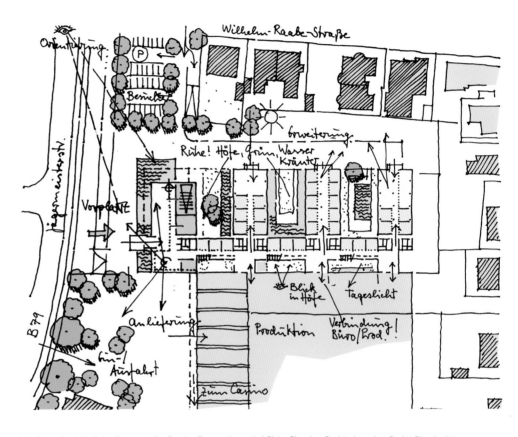

Left: Reception hall. Links: Eingangshalle. Gauche: Espace d'accueil. | Right: Site plan. Rechts: Lageplan. Droite: Plan du site.

The cordial liquor manufacturer wanted a new building that could react rationally and flexibly to future business reorganization, and simultaneously satisfy the demand for quality work space. A reversible office concept with organizational flexibility was born, whose four-story office wings in the shape of an open comb form a scaled transition to the surrounding low-standing residential city structures. The administrative building is tightly connected to the previously existing production area through its location, melting into one structural volume. Functionally, separate and clearly-defined areas with various, exciting elements like walkways, paths, look-outs and "spy holes" are created.

Der Likörhersteller wünschte einen Neubau, der das flexible Reagieren auf veränderte Organisationsstrukturen zulässt und die Anforderungen an einen qualitätsvollen Arbeitsplatz erfüllt. Es entstand ein reversibles Bürokonzept mit anpassungsfähigen Bürobereichen. Viergeschossige, wie ein offener Kamm angeordnete Büroflügel bilden einen stufenweisen Übergang zu der umliegenden Wohnbebauung. Das Verwaltungsgebäude ist durch seine Lage mit dem bestehenden Produktionsbereich eng verbunden und verschmilzt mit ihm zu einem einzigen Bauvolumen. Das Resultat sind funktionell unabhängige und eindeutig definierte Zonen mit spannenden Elementen wie Gängen, Ausblicken und „Gucklöchern".

Le client – un fabriquant de liqueur – souhaitait un immeuble doté d'une atmosphère de travail de qualité et capable de s'adapter à la réorganisation future de l'entreprise. Les architectes ont par conséquent élaboré un projet caractérisé par sa flexibilité. L'immeuble de quatre étages en forme de peigne réalise une transition progressive avec les bâtiments résidentiels bas construits aux alentours. Le nouvel immeuble de bureaux est étroitement connecté au bâtiment de production préexistant, de sorte que les deux volumes n'en forment plus qu'un. Les espaces intérieurs, aux fonctions clairement définies, se complètent par divers éléments surprenants, notamment des judas optiques.

From left to right, from above to below:
View toward entrance hall,
fully glazed façade, bridge at entrance, sculpture.
Right: Lobby.

Von links nach rechts, von oben nach unten:
Blick Richtung Eingangshalle,
verglaste Fassade, Brücke am Eingang, Skulptur.
Rechts: Empfangsbereich.

De gauche à droite, de haut en bas:
Vue sur le hall d'entrée,
façade entièrement vitrée, rampe à l'entrée, sculpture.
Droite: Espace d'accueil.

# ARTE HEADQUARTERS,
## STRASBOURG, FRANCE

STRUHK ARCHITEKTEN
PLANUNGSGSELLSCHAFT MBH

www.struhk.de
**Client:** ARTE G.E.I.E, **Completion:** 2003, **Gross floor area:** 23,500 m², **Photos:** Courtesy of struhk architekten.

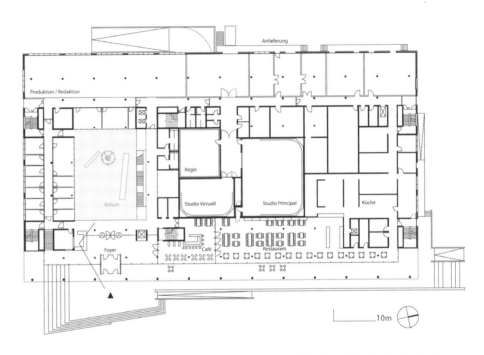

Left: East façade by night. Links: Ostfassade bei Nacht. Gauche: Façade est de nuit. | Right: Ground floor plan. Rechts: Grundriss Erdgeschoss. Droite: Plan du rez-de-chaussée.

The four-story compact building structure developed from the complex functional requirements. The elevated ground level houses the studios with high ceilings surrounded by a circle of editing, production and technical rooms, as well as the restaurant facing the river. The two office floors, including production and office areas, extend over the elevated ground and are arranged around the glass-covered four-story atrium and a garden yard on the third floor. Transparency between the indoors and outdoors is in line with the self-image of the broadcasting station.

Der viergeschossige kompakte Baukörper entwickelt sich aus den komplexen funktionalen Anforderungen. Im Sockelgeschoss befinden sich die Studios mit großen Raumhöhen umgeben von einem Kranz aus Regie-, Produktions- und Technikräumen sowie dem zum Fluss orientierten Restaurant. Die über das Sockelgeschoss auskragenden beiden Bürogeschosse mit Produktions- und Büroräumen sind um das glasgedeckte viergeschossige Atrium und einen Gartenhof im dritten Obergeschoss angeordnet. Transparenz zwischen Innen und Außen entspricht dem Selbstverständnis der Sendeanstalt.

Cet immeuble compact de quatre étages a été conçu pour remplir des fonctions complexes. Au rez-de-chaussée se trouvent des studios hauts de plafond, entourés des salles de technique et de production, ainsi que d'un restaurant avec vue sur la rivière. Deux étages de bureaux, en surplomb au-dessus du rez-de-chaussée, entourent une verrière sur quatre niveaux complétée par un jardin intérieur situé au troisième étage. La transparence du bâtiment correspond à la philosophie de la chaîne de télévision Arte.

From left to right, from above to below:
Reception, entrance hall,
conference room, four-story entrance hall.
Right: Glazed atrium.

Von links nach rechts, von oben nach unten:
Empfang, Eingangshalle,
Konferenzraum, vier-geschossige Eingangshalle.
Rechts: Verglastes Atrium.

De gauche à droite, de haut en bas:
Réception, hall d'entrée, salle de conférence,
vue des 4 étages depuis le hall d'entrée.
Droite: Atrium entièrement vitré.

# STUDIO BACIOCCHI &
# PRADA HEADQUARTERS,
## AREEZO, ITALY

# STUDIO BACIOCCHI SRL

www.baciocchi.it
Client: Studio Baciocchi – Prada, **Completion:** 2001, **Gross floor area:** 8,500 m², **Photos:** Andrea Rum.

Left: Second floor, staircase and elevator. Links: Zweite Etage, Treppe und Fahrstuhl. Gauche: 2e étage, escalier et ascenseur. | Right: Third floor plan. Rechts: Grundriss dritte Etage. Droite: Plan du 3e étage.

An existing austere, simple concrete building was modified and reinterpreted to create a structure devoted exclusively to work offices. The place emphasizes the flexible and minimal nature of the space. Framed aluminum and translucent polycarbonate panels separate various work areas. The electrical and mechanical systems are attached to the undersides of floor slabs. All furnishings were designed and executed specifically for the offices. The compact three-story building houses the general services on the ground floor, and individual work stations, meeting rooms, workshops and teamwork areas on the upper floors.

Ein nüchterner, einfacher Betonbau wurde für eine ausschließliche Büronutzung umgestaltet und neu interpretiert. Der Ort unterstreicht die flexible und minimalistische Ausstattung der Räume. Aluminiumrahmen mit transparenten Polycarbonatplatten trennen die verschiedenen Arbeitsbereiche voneinander. Die Versorgungssysteme sind an den Deckenunterseiten befestigt. Alle Einrichtungsgegenstände wurden eigens für die Büros entworfen und hergestellt. In dem kompakten dreigeschossigen Gebäude befinden sich die allgemeinen Serviceflächen im Erdgeschoss. Einzelarbeitsplätze, Besprechungsräume sowie Zonen für Workshops und Teamarbeit sind in den oberen Stockwerken untergebracht.

Un austère bâtiment en béton a été réaménagé et transformé en immeuble de bureaux. Les architectes ont mis l'accent sur la flexibilité et le minimalisme. Des panneaux en matière plastique translucide garnis de cadres en aluminium séparent les divers espaces de travail. Les équipements mécaniques et électriques sont visibles au plafond. Tous les meubles de bureau ont été spécialement réalisés. Dans cet immeuble compact, les espaces de service sont regroupés au rez-de-chaussée, tandis que les bureaux, les ateliers, les salles de réunion et les salles de travail en équipe se répartissent sur les deux autres étages.

Concrete façade. Betonfassade. Façade en béton.

From left to right, from above to below:
Hallway, conference room,
glazed skylight, polycarbonate panels.
Right: Cafeteria at ground floor.

Von links nach rechts, von oben nach unten:
Flur, Tagungsraum, verglastes Oberlicht,
Polykarbonatpaneele.
Rechts: Cafeteria im Erdgeschoss.

De gauche à droite, de haut en bas:
Couloir, salle de conférence, plafond vitré,
panneaux de polycarbonate.
Droite: Cafétéria au rez-de-chaussée.

# MARCONI COMMUNICATIONS CORPORATE CAMPUS,
## WARRENDALE, PA, USA

# STUDIOS ARCHITECTURE

www.studiosarch.com
**Client:** Marconi Communications, **Completion:** 2003, **Gross floor area:** 113,000 sq. ft., **Photos:** Edward Massery Photography.

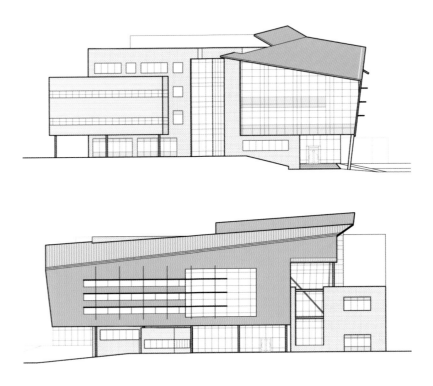

Left: Copper coated façade. Links: Kupferbeschichtete Fassade. Gauche: Façade avec panneaux en cuivre. | Right: Sections. Rechts: Schnitte. Droite: Coupes.

The design for this six-building campus needed to evoke a sense of community since employees typically remain on the grounds throughout the workday. The design emphasizes circulation and incorporates interior and exterior common areas to encourage interaction between employees. Open stair lobbies create visual connections between floors, and enclosed pedestrian spine encourages travel between buildings. The new complex features office, research and development facilities, a light assembly space, a large, multi-purpose dining facility and parking for 1,000 employees.

Da die Mitarbeiter ihren Arbeitstag meistens auf dem Gelände verbringen, sollte der Entwurf für die Anlage mit sechs Gebäuden den Gemeinschaftssinn wecken. Infolgedessen sind die Wegeführung akzentuiert und zur Förderung der Kommunikation sind innen und außen Gemeinschaftsflächen angeordnet. Offene Treppenhallen schaffen visuelle Verbindungen zwischen den einzelnen Geschossen, und eine geschlossene Erschließungsachse ermuntert zum Pendeln zwischen den Gebäuden. Der neue Komplex beherbergt Büros, Forschungs- und Entwicklungseinrichtungen, einen Versammlungsraum, einen vielseitig nutzbaren Speisesaal und Parkplätze für 1.000 Mitarbeiter.

En réalisant ces six bâtiments hospitaliers, les architectes ont cherché à promouvoir l'esprit d'équipe du personnel – une nécessité puisque les employés passent toute leur journée ici. Le complexe met en valeur la circulation et inclut divers espaces conviviaux situés tant à l'intérieur qu'à l'extérieur des bâtiments. Les cages d'escaliers ouvertes favorisent les contacts d'un étage à l'autre, tandis que des passages couverts facilitent les déplacements entre les différents immeubles. Le complexe inclut des bureaux, des laboratoires de recherche, une salle de réunion, une grande salle polyvalente et un parking de mille places.

From left to right, from above to below:
Side view, view toward entrance, workstations.
Right: Exterior view.

Von links nach rechts, von oben nach unten:
Seitenansicht, Blick Richtung Eingang, Arbeitsplätze.
Rechts: Außenansicht.

De gauche à droite, de haut en bas:
Vue latérale, vue sur l'entrée, espaces de travail.
Droite: Vue extérieure.

# BARCLAYS GLOBAL INVESTORS HEADQUARTERS,
## SAN FRANCISCO, CA, USA

# STUDIOS ARCHITECTURE

www.studiosarch.com

**Client:** Barclays Global Investors, **Completion:** 2008, **Gross floor area:** 380,000 sq. ft., **Photos:** Benny Chan / Fotoworks.

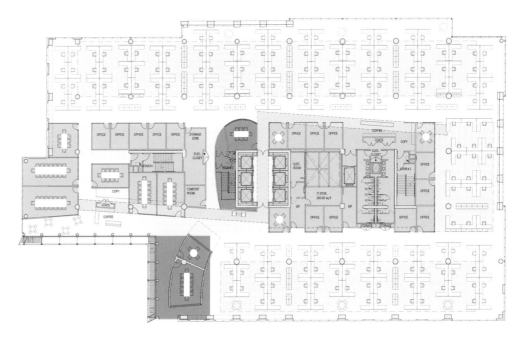

Left: Entrance hall. Links: Eingangshalle. Gauche: Hall d'entrée. | **Right: Typical floor plan.** Rechts: Regelgeschoss. Droite: Plan caractéristique.

The building is part of a four-building complex. Its design includes a central conference and break area zone, which connects the primary collaborative zones to the vertical circulation zones. The large flexible open floor plan can adapt to Barclays' changing needs. The ten-story headquarters includes 60,000 sq. ft. of trading floor space and a large roof deck for the use of Barclays' staff and clients. The design is influenced by Barclays' core principles of research and innovation, resulting in a collaborative and dynamic environment that promotes communication and fosters creativity.

Das Gebäude gehört zu einem Komplex aus vier Bauten. Sein Entwurf umfasst einen zentralen Konferenz- und Pausenbereich, der zwischen den wichtigsten kooperativen Flächen und den vertikalen Erschließungszonen vermittelt. Der flexible offene Grundriss lässt sich an Barclays wechselnde Bedürfnisse anpassen. Die zehngeschossige Verwaltungszentrale verfügt über eine Geschäftsfläche von 5.575 m² sowie über eine ausgedehnte Dachveranda für Barclays' Mitarbeiter und Kunden. Aus dem von Barclays' Grundprinzipien der Forschung und Innovation beeinflussten Entwurf resultiert ein kooperatives und dynamisches Arbeitsumfeld, das die Kommunikation fördert und zur Kreativität anregt.

Cet immeuble fait partie d'un ensemble de quatre bâtiments. On y trouve une salle de conférence et une zone de repos située à l'intersection des espaces collectifs et des zones de circulation verticale. Les architectes ont opté pour un plan modulable permettant au client de réaménager l'intérieur en fonction de ses besoins. Le siège social de Barclay se compose ainsi d'environ vingt mille mètres carrés de bureaux répartis sur dix étages, auxquels s'ajoute le toit en terrasse accessible aux employés et aux clients. Les aménagements reflètent l'intérêt de la banque pour la recherche et l'innovation, avec pour résultat un environnement dynamique qui favorise la communication et la créativité.

Conference room. Tagungsraum. Salle de conférence.

From left to right, from above to below:
Meeting area, open office spaces, conference room.
Right: Workstations.

Von links nach rechts, von oben nach unten:
Aufenthaltsraum, offene Bürolandschaft, Tagungsraum.
Rechts: Arbeitsplätze.

De gauche à droite, de haut en bas:
Vue sur la salle d'accueil, espaces libres de travail,
salle de conférence.
Droite: Espace de travail.

# BEA SYSTEMS REGIONAL OFFICE,
## SAN FRANCISCO, CA, USA

# STUDIOS ARCHITECTURE

www.studiosarch.com

**Client:** BEA Systems, **Completion:** 2007, **Gross floor area:** 110,000 m², **Photos:** Benny Chan / Fotoworks.

Left: View of conference room from lobby. Links: Ansicht vom Tagungsraum aus der Lobby. Gauche: Vue depuis l'accueil sur la salle de conférence. | Right: Floor Plan. Rechts: Grundriss. Droite: Plan.

The design includes an executive briefing center, executive offices, open plan research and development offices, and a break area. A stairway links all six floors, and a second staircase connects the executive offices to the executive briefing center. The result is simple and flexible, with a very contemporary feeling. STUDIOS created many meeting opportunities, both formal and informal, to foster the relationships among employees. Elements such as maple wood furniture add warmth to the light and airy space, while glass-walled interior offices and conference rooms promote transparency and openness.

Zum Entwurf gehören ein Executive Briefing Center, Büros für Führungskräfte, Forschungs- und Entwicklungsbüros mit offenem Grundriss sowie ein Pausenbereich. Eine Treppe erschließt alle sechs Geschosse, eine weitere stellt die Verbindung zwischen den Büros der Geschäftsleitung und dem Executive Briefing Center her. Das Ergebnis ist einfach und flexibel bei einem höchst modernen Ambiente. Um die Beziehungen zwischen den Angestellten zu fördern, schuf STUDIOS Möglichkeiten für formelle und informelle Begegnungen. Ahornmöbel bringen Behaglichkeit in den hellen und luftigen Raum. Dagegen verstärken die Glaswände der inneren Büros und Konferenzzimmer die Transparenz und Offenheit.

Cet immeuble inclut les bureaux de la direction, ceux du département de recherche et développement, ainsi qu'une zone de repos. Un premier escalier interconnecte les six étages, tandis qu'un second relie les bureaux de la direction à une salle de réunion. L'ensemble se caractérise par sa simplicité, sa flexibilité et son atmosphère contemporaine. Afin de favoriser la communication entre les employés, les architectes ont aussi conçu plusieurs espaces réservés aux réunions formelles ou informelles. Les aménagements intérieurs en érable contribuent à l'impression générale de chaleur et de clarté, tandis que des cloisons en verre suggèrent la transparence et l'ouverture.

Reception and communicating stair. Empfang und Treppe für Kommunikation. Réception et escalier reliant les étages.

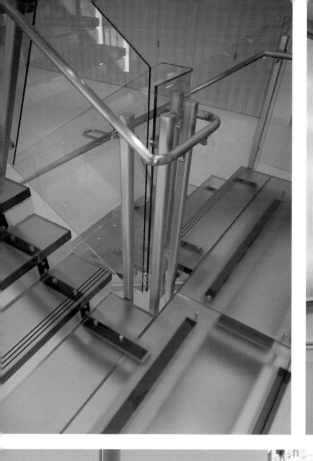

From left to right, from above to below:
Detail stair, office space, workstation.
Right: Glass and steel stair.

Von links nach rechts, von oben nach unten:
Treppendetail, Bürolandschaft, Arbeitsplatz.
Rechts: Treppe aus Glas und Stahl.

De gauche à droite, de haut en bas:
Détail de l'escalier, espace de travail, bureaux.
Droite: Escalier de verre et d'acier.

# DEPARTMENT OF HEALTH SERVICES,
## RICHMOND, CA, USA

www.studiosarch.com

Client: State of California, Completion: 2005, Gross floor area: 200,000 sq. ft., Photos: Tim Griffith.

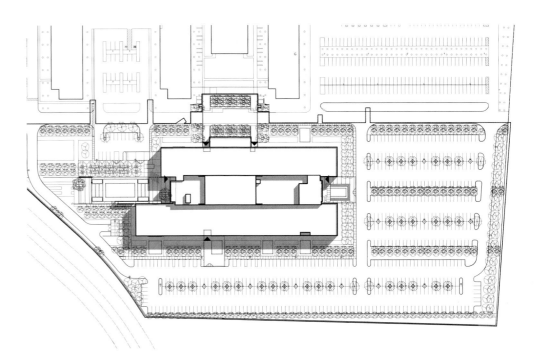

Left: Entry courtyard. Links: Eingang Innenhof. Gauche: Entrée de la cour intérieure. | Right: Site plan. Rechts: Lageplan. Droite: Plan du site.

The building´s large-scale linearity and extruded forms establish a common identity with its two existing companion structures while still making a unique visual statement. The entry courtyard, which features a sculpture garden with a sunken grass court and public seating, creates a significant and welcoming space for visitors and employees through its architecture and its landscape. Beyond the entryway, a central atrium feeds natural light into the building and serves as a community gathering space for DHS functions ranging from group staff meetings to all-hands assemblies.

Die ausgeprägte Geradlinigkeit und die langgestreckten Formen dieses Gebäudes begründen zusammen mit den beiden Nachbarbauten eine gemeinsame Identität. Dennoch hat es einen eigenen sichtbaren Ausdruck. Der Eingangshof mit einem Skulpturengarten nebst einem vertieften Rasenplatz und öffentlichen Sitzgelegenheiten heißt mit seiner Landschaft und Architektur Besucher und Mitarbeiter willkommen. Hinter dem Zugang bringt ein zentrales Atrium natürliches Licht in das Gebäude. Es ist für DHS-Veranstaltungen bestimmt, von Gruppentreffen bis zu Mitarbeiterversammlungen.

Par son caractère linaire et monumental, cet édifice s'intègre parfaitement à son environnement immédiat tout en affirmant sa propre identité. Des sculptures, des bancs et une pelouse créent une atmosphère accueillante aux abords du bâtiment. Le hall d'entrée est couvert par une verrière qui optimise l'éclairage naturel. Il peut être utilisé pour les réunions des employés et les assemblées générales.

From left to right, from above to below:
Exit stair at west entry, view of workstations
from central light court, east entry, façade.
Right: Central light court.

Von links nach rechts, von oben nach unten:
Außentreppe am Westeingang,
Blick aus dem Lichthof auf die Arbeitsplätze,
Osteingang, Fassade.
Rechts: Zentraler Lichthof.

De gauche à droite, de haut en bas:
Escalier extérieur situé vers l'entrée ouest,
vue sur l'espace de travail, entrée est, façade.
Droite: Cour centrale lumineuse.

# ORRICK, HERRINGTON &
# SUTCLIFFE LAW OFFICE,
## SAN FRANCISCO, CA, USA

www.studiosarch.com

Client: Orrick Herrington & Sutcliffe LLP San Francisco Office, Completion: 2004, Gross floor area: 164,000 sq. ft., Photos: Benny Chan / Fotoworks (284, 286 a.r.), Tim Griffith (286 a.l., 286 b., 287).

Left: Entrance hall. Links: Eingangshalle. Gauche: Hall d'entrée. | Right: Seventh floor plan. Rechts: Grundriss Siebte Etage. Droite: Plan du 7e étage.

The 150-year-old law firm asked STUDIOS to redesign its offices to suit the needs of a modern law practice and to update its corporate identity. The concept accentuates the virtues of the building, such as its roofline, its canted volumes in contrast with rectilinear forms, and its transparent glass skin, which provides a panoramic view and fills the interior with natural light. Striated and gridded patterns are repeated on the windows, floor plans and ceilings. The design added a modern interpretation of wood paneling and stone – the materials typically associated with institutional architecture.

Die 150 Jahre alte Anwaltskanzlei beauftragte STUDIOS mit der Neugestaltung ihrer Büros, um sie der heutigen anwaltlichen Tätigkeit anzupassen. Darüber hinaus sollte ihre Corporate Identity auf den neuesten Stand gebracht werden. Das Konzept akzentuiert die Vorzüge des Gebäudes wie seine Dachsilhouette, seine abgeschrägten Volumen im Gegensatz zu geradlinigen Formen und seine transparente Glashaut, die eine Panoramaaussicht gewährt und die Innenräume mit natürlichem Licht erfüllt. Streifen- und Gittermuster wiederholen sich an Fenstern, Grundrissen und Decken. Hinzu kamen eine modern interpretierte Holztäfelung und Stein.

Le client – un cabinet d'avocats fondé il y a plus d'un siècle et demi – a demandé aux architectes de concevoir un siège social correspondant à la nouvelle image de l'entreprise. Le concept retenu met en valeur les qualités du bâtiment, notamment la forme du toit, les lignes brisées qui rompent la linéarité et l'enveloppe transparente qui assure un bon éclairage naturel de l'intérieur tout en offrant des vues panoramiques des environs. Des lignes parallèles se retrouvent sur les fenêtres, les plafonds et le plancher. Le bâtiment dans son ensemble réinterprète deux matériaux typiques de l'architecture traditionnelle: le bois et la pierre.

# MERCADO DESIGN,
## BRASÍLIA, BRAZIL

# TAO ARQUITETURA

www.pauloheriqueparanhos.com
**Client:** Faustino Porto, **Completion:** 2007, **Gross floor area:** 2,600 m², **Photos:** TAO Arquitetura, Telmo Ximensi.

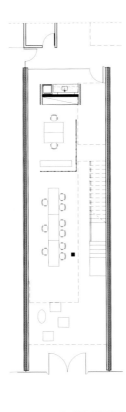

Left: Reception. Links: Empfang. Gauche: Réception. | Right: Ground floor plan. Rechts: Grundriss Erdgeschoss. Droite: Plan du rez-de-chaussée.

The Mercado Design project is born from the understanding of the building using a number of concepts: a single flat volume with considerable permeability that is able to provoke the effect of surprise. At first glance, it presents more of a challenge than an explicit revelation. It is not intended to sell material goods, but rather to discuss motivations that lead people to search for bigger values, to desire a better quality of life. The design hopes to aim at something that is not limited to palpable issues, but can rather suggest a wider perception.

Das Projekt Mercado Design beruht auf mehreren Konzepten, die in das Gebäude einfließen. Ein einziges flaches, sehr durchlässiges Volumen kann einen Überraschungseffekt auslösen. Auf den ersten Blick ist es mehr eine Herausforderung als eine Enthüllung. Es soll keine materiellen Güter verkaufen, sondern Motivationen diskutieren, die Menschen veranlassen, nach höheren Werten zu suchen, eine bessere Lebensqualität zu wünschen. Der Entwurf zielt auf etwas ab, das sich nicht auf offenkundige Themen beschränkt. Vielmehr möchte er eine umfassendere Wahrnehmung nahelegen.

Ce volume unique hautement perméable utilise divers concept et provoque un effet de surprise. À première vue, ce « marché » n'est pas très explicite et semble être une gageure. C'est probablement dû au fait qu'on n'y vend pas des biens matériels, mais qu'on s'y rencontre pour discuter des possibilités d'améliorer la qualité de vie. Le style architectural choisi exprime ainsi la volonté de s'éloigner du palpable pour jouir d'une perception élargie.

From left to right, from above to below:
Interior, showroom, detail stair, sileston stair.
Right: Front view.

Von links nach rechts, von oben nach unten:
Innenansicht, Verkaufsraum,
Treppendetail, Treppe aus Sileston.
Rechts: Fassadenansicht.

De gauche à droite, de haut en bas:
Intérieur, salle d'exposition,
détail de l'escalier, escalier en sileston.
Droite: Vue de devant.

# SELIMEX,
## LATSCH, ITALY

# WERNER TSCHOLL ARCHITEKT

www.wernertscholl.com

**Client:** Selimex GmbH, Walter Rizzi, **Completion:** 2005, **Gross floor area:** 900 m², **Photos:** Alexa Rainer.

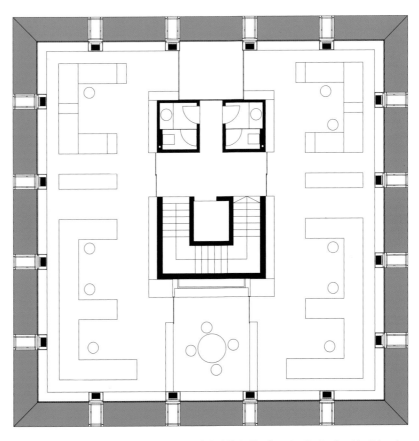

Left: **Side view.** Links: Seitenansicht. Gauche: Vue latérale. | Right: **First floor plan.** Rechts: Grundriss Erdgeschoss. Droite: Plan du rez-de-chaussée.

The structure of this building is a completely glazed parallele piped emerging form water, characterized on the sides by likewise glazed volumes protruding horizontally and vertically. The proximity of surfaces of different nature and consistence creates a continual interplay of reflections enlivening the architectonic object. If by day the green glass blends perfectly with the surroundings of the site, and the light filling the building from the outside, at night the building becomes an object emanating continuously changing colors.

Das Gebäude besteht aus einem vollständig verglasten Quader, der aus dem Wasser aufsteigt. Charakteristisch sind die an seinen Seiten vertikal und horizontal hervortretenden, ebenfalls gläsernen Volumen. Benachbarte Flächen unterschiedlicher Art und Konsistenz erzeugen ein ständiges Wechselspiel von Reflexionen, die den Baukörper mit Leben erfüllen. Tagsüber verschmilzt das grüne Glas vortrefflich mit der Umgebung des Standorts, und die Konstruktion wird von außen mit Licht erfüllt. Nachts gerät das Gebäude zu einem Objekt, das unablässig wechselnde Farben hervorbringt.

Cet immeuble est un cube entièrement vitré posé sur un plan d'eau, avec une structure porteuse de barres horizontales et verticales protubérantes. Un dynamisme particulier résulte de l'interaction de plusieurs surfaces de nature et de consistance différentes. La couleur verte de la structure et des plaques de verre s'harmonise parfaitement au site naturel dans la journée, tandis que l'ensemble change constamment de couleur durant de la nuit.

From left to right, from above to below:
Detail staircase, street side view, art gallery on the ground floor,
luminescented building.
Right: Exterior view by night.

Von links nach rechts, von oben nach unten:
Treppendetail, Blick von der Straße, Kunstgallerie im Erdgeschoss,
leuchtendes Gebäude.
Rechts: Außenansicht bei Nacht.

De gauche à droite, de haut en bas:
Détail de l'escalier, vue de la rue, galerie d'art au rez-de-chaussée,
bâtiment illuminé.
Droite: Vue de nuit.

# REHAUWORK,
## REHAU, GERMANY

www.weberwuerschinger.com

**Client:** REHAU AG & CO., **Completion:** 2004, **Gross floor area:** 3.200 m², **Photographer:** Marcus Weidlich.

Left: Open workspaces. Links: Offene Bürolandschaft. Gauche: Espaces de travail. | Right: Floor plans. Rechts: Grundrisse. Droite: Plans.

On an area of 3,200 m² of a former porcelain plant, the architects created offices for managers, work spaces for 150 employees, printer and copier zones, meeting spaces and alternative work spaces, a break and exhibition space, and plenty of storage room for samples. The architects developed a color and materials scheme reduced to the colors grey and white, reflecting the properties and color of porcelain as a raw material. Colorful accents are added by orange felt areas and planted sections. The flooring of the entire office space consists of solid oak floorboards.

Auf 3.200 m² einer ehemalige Porzellanfabrik brachten die Architekten Abteilungsleiterbüros, Arbeitsplätze für 150 Mitarbeiter, Zonen für Drucker und Kopierer, Besprechungsbereiche und Ausweicharbeitsplätze, eine Pausen- und Ausstellungszone und viel Stauraum für Musterteile unter. Die Architekten entwickelten ein auf die Farben grau und weiß reduziertes Farb- und Materialkonzept, in dem sich der Werkstoff Porzellan in seiner Beschaffenheit und Farbe reflektiert. Für farbliche Akzente sorgen schließlich orangefarbene Filzflächen und Pflanzenflächen. Im gesamten Bürobereich besteht der Boden aus massiven Eichendielen.

Les architectes ont transformé une ancienne fabrique de porcelaine couvrant 3200 mètres carrés en un immeuble de bureaux pour cent cinquante employés. On y trouve des salles de réunion, de repos et d'exposition, ainsi que des espaces de stockage et des locaux pour imprimantes et photocopieuses. La gamme de couleurs de tous les matériaux utilisés, réduite au blanc et au gris, rappelle l'utilisation antérieure des locaux. Des plantes vertes et des quelques zones de couleur orange viennent néanmoins rehausser cette palette volontairement minimaliste. Tous les bureaux sont pourvus de parquet en chêne massif.

Meeting room. Aufenthaltsraum. Hall d'accueil.

From left to right, from above to below:
Interior, workspaces, illuminated
"hayfield", detail illumination.
Right: Conference table.

Von links nach rechts, von oben nach unten:
Inneneinrichtung, Arbeitsplätze,
"Lichtwiese", Beleuchtungsdetail.
Rechts: Konferenztisch.

De gauche à droite, de haut en bas:
Intérieur, espaces de travail,
„pelouse" illuminée, détail des illuminations.
Droite: Table de conférence.

**INDEX.**

Imprint

The Deutsche Bibliothek lists this publication in the Deutsche Nationalbiblio-
graphie; detailed bibliographical information are available on the internet
at http://dnb.ddb.de

ISBN 978-3-03768-007-0

© 2009 by Braun Publishing AG

2nd edition 2011

Project coordinator: Annika Schulz
Editorial staff: Dagmar Glück
Translation: Claire Chamot, Marcel Saché, Cosima Talhouni,
Joanna Zajac-Heinken
Lektorat: Cosima Talhouni
Graphic concept and layout: Michaela Prinz